LETTERS
TO THE EDITOR

From the Trenches of Democracy

Volume 6

President Obama's Legacy vs.
America - Final Round 8

America lost everything

WORLD UNDER ATTACK

BY

RADICAL ISLAMIC TERRORISM

The 2016 Presidential Elections
Doom or Deliverance?
Hillary Clinton vs. Donald Trump

By

DANIEL B. JEFFS

ISBN: 1508703825
ISBN 13: 9781508703822

DELIVERANCE !

President Donald Trump

Concluding letters to the editor below:

San Diego Union-Tribune
March 27, 2017

Letting Obamacare implode is right course

It is best that President Trump House Republicans did not have the votes to repeal and replace Obamacare. Indeed, the Unaffordable Careless Act has been well on the road to imploding, as it was destined to do, particularly when it was rammed through the Democrat-controlled Congress from behind closed doors. As incompetent House Speaker, Nancy Pelosi said, "We have to pass it so we will know what's in it."

Surely, after the ACA implodes, the Republican must get their act together and pass enough legislation to help the nation's health care industry get back on its feet and help the American people recover. A good start would be to allow insurance companies to sell health insurance across state lines.

Alas, President Obama's painful legacy will continue to implode and explode as time goes on.

VV Daily Press
March 24, 2017

CBO must go for cooking the books

When President Obama and the Democrat Congress rammed through the phony Unaffordable Careless Act laden with Obama's lies, America's health care was turned upside down and inside out at terrible, unnecessary cost and confusion. An insidious legacy to say the least. Of course, it was substantially the result of the Democrats' puppet OBM and passage from behind doors closed to Republicans – then upheld by a weak Supreme Court.

Now, with the election of President Donald Trump and a Republican-controlled Congress, the prosed repeal of ObamaCareless -- to be replaced with the American Health Care Act -- and the opposing bias of the OMB warning leaving 24 million Americans uninsured, something has to go.

Indeed, the Congressional Budget Office should be eliminated and replaced with private professional budget analysist experts who will provide honest reports instead of the deeply imbedded bureaucrats who have been conditioned to give liberals what they want. And that goes for all Washington bureaucrats who must get their acts together, or leave.

VV Daily Press
March 19, 2017

The hounds of Democrats

Since Donald Trump's election and his concentrated efforts to deliver on his promises to the American people, President Obama, Hillary Clinton and their minions in and out of government – supported by billionaire, George Soros – have launched their "Hounds of Democrats" against President Trump, The Republican Congress and all good, patriotic Americans with a vengeance.

Indeed, President (Premier) Obama's early learning in Communism and the long-term Clinton corruption machine have come to fruition in gathering the storm to undermine and destroy President Trump, his administration and the Congress at any cost. Clearly, the enemy within is alive with social, political and economic sabotage and cancers to accomplish their treasonous madness.

Nevertheless, with God's help, President Trump and true Americans will prevail against all enemies, foreign and domestic.

Daniel B. Jeffs

President Trump delivers

President Trump's February 28th address to Congress was clearly presidential and optimistic, outlining his policies to deliver the strongest domestic, border and national security, lower taxes on job-creating businesses and the middle-class, repair the nation's infrastructure -- repeal the Unaffordable Careless Act and replace it with workable health care -- create jobs, cut the overwhelming size and over-regulations imposed by government – and improve political divisions.

Coupled with overhauling public education, restoring the coal industry, approving the Keystone Pipeline with American steel, insisting on fair trade and keeping jobs in America, backing law enforcement and the military completely with increased forces, weapons and equipment – restoring and increasing our nuclear weapon power and defenses, restoring and improving our relations with NATO, and destroying ISIS, President Trump is in the process of delivering what he promised the American people.

Indeed, the president will attack terrorism and crime on every front, including drug cartels and criminal illegal aliens until American is safe. Clearly, President Trump is moving ahead to provide deliverance from 8 years of doom from President Obama and the continued doom of a president Hillary Clinton.

Daniel B. Jeffs
March 1, 2017

Obama's doom to Trump's deliverance

After 8 years of suffering from President Obama's "Demoncrat" empire of corruption, overwhelming rules, regulations, economic damages, education indoctrination and Pravda-style news media, the American people patriots were ready for a complete change of government leadership.

Coupled with Obama-caused deepening racial and political divisions, the war against police, the unchecked rise of ISIS terrorism and the dangers to our domestic and national security, President Obama was narrowly re-elected and Republicans gained majority control of House in 2012.

Indeed, with the 2016 presidential election looming continued doom with Democrat Hillary Clinton's nomination, Republican Donald Trump was nominated and won decisively -- and control of the Senate -- with the rise of the silent majority of true Americans -- and embarked on the difficult journey to deliver us from evil.

In response, marching orders were given to activist "Demoncrats" in the Democrat Party and declared war on President Trump and Congressional Republicans with constant massive, aggressive street protests and demands to hold town hall meetings in Congressional districts.

Undeterred, President Trump is moving forward to repeal and replace Obama's Unaffordable Health Care Act and Dodd-Frank finance act fiasco, boost our economy, protect our borders, stop the war on police and eliminate ISIS and to restore and increase our domestic and national security.

Furthermore, President Trump will restore President Obama's dangerous cuts in our military strength – which also reduced our nuclear weapons to well below Russia's – to maintain overwhelming strength as a deterrent to any nuclear attacks by Russia, North Korea or any country with nuclear weapons including Iran.

Recommended reading: *Worst President in History: The Legacy of Barack Obama (contains 200 reasons)*, by Matt Margolis & Mark Noonan

Daniel B. Jeffs
February 25, 2017

VV Daily Press
February 17, 2017

Democrats vs. Republicans

Leftist liberal Democrats are making it painfully clear that they are waging a war of political terrorism against newly-elected President Trump, conservative patriots and the Republican Congress, with relentless personal attacks, mass demonstrations, protests and riots throughout the country, especially in California.

Indeed, with our Constitution, freedoms and liberty at stake, this reckless behavior is becoming a crisis bordering on all-out war, tantamount to treason. Clearly, insidious leaders such as George Soros, Unions, the miseducation establishment, the Pravda-style news media, socialists, extremists and Democrat bosses in the House and Senate are driving the effort with the runaway tyranny of big government and political correctness.

Certainly, the reason behind the upheaval is the time bomb President Obama built over 8 years with his war against police and the rise of Black Lives Matte,, the proliferation of ISIS by ignoring their rapid Middle East and world-wide aggression, and the increases of illegal aliens, crime, drugs and refugees.

Coupled with Mr. Obama's and the Democrat Congress' expansion of intrusive government and control of healthcare, finance and the economy, he has assumed the position of leadership of the indoctrinated enemy within, lit the fuse and left office to ruin America.

Daniel B. Jeffs
February 17, 2017

Conclusion of Obama's presidency

Barack Obama's presidency was a disaster in determined motion, leaving America with the ongoing results of the political left's long term goal of undermining our constitutional republic's freedoms and protections – accomplished through miseducation indoctrination and political tyranny, supported by left-wing news media.

Indeed, our unique democracy has suffered serious damage at the hands of the unrelenting enemy within, which will continue until the true patriotic citizenry of the right wins the many-sided conflicts with the left.

Fortunately, the left's Hillary Clinton was defeated by the right's Donald Trump in the 2016 presidential election, which avoided doom, and provided a way to deliverance supported by the right's increased influence in the Congress.

Unfortunately, the left's response to President Trump has been hostile and vitriolic, with incessant street protests and demonstrations, some violent, exacerbated by the insidious Pravda-style totalitarian -- nit-picking national media.

Fortunately, we have the counter-force integrity of Fox News, the Wall Street Journal, the Washington Times, NewsMax Magazine and enough local and regional news media – all fair, balanced and unafraid to defend liberty....

Daniel B. Jeffs
February 10, 2017

Devil's triangle: Obama, Hillary and Soros

Since President Obama's reign began, America has been beset by an insidious inverted pentagram comprised of a socialist Democrat Congress, and radical leftist activists bent on the destruction of America with a goat head devil's triangle at the center with images of hate-crusaders President Obama, Hillary Clinton and George Soros at the root of devastating intentions and doom.

Fortunately, the patriotic conservative core of Constitutional American people and voters elected Republican Donald Trump president in 2016, and increased control of a Republican Congress to save our nation and "Make America Great Again."

Unfortunately, the devil's triangle and their hostile, often violent, followers will be laboring to undermine President Trump, his administration and the Republican Congress to tear down everything until America falls into the oblivion of traitors and terrorists determined to rule the world with a bloody sword.

However, hail to the chief -- We will survive, win and prosper. Indeed, God bless America to save us from what has become a superficial society of social aggression, selfish interests, political tyranny, radicals, indoctrination and extremes at the hands of evil. Alas, God will provide deliverance from evil....

Daniel B. Jeffs
February 7, 2017

DEDICATION

To my fellow letter writers

America at the crossroads: Doom or Deliverance?

As America celebrates the legacy of Dr. Martin Luther King, we struggle with the 2017 outgoing legacy of President Barrack Obama, our first African American president, and what he has wrought upon our nation – certainly not in the tradition of Dr. King. Indeed, America is at the perilous crossroads of the tearing down our country and our recovery with the incoming president, Donald Trump. Alas, that's not racism, it's a stark reality….

Surely, if nothing else, it has become painfully clear that our survival depends entirely upon the outcome of a war between good and evil in the sense of what has always been the greatness of America and those who thrive on attacking our fundamental good – the things that set us apart from the evils within our society that we must deal with based upon our founding principles of freedom. self-determination, liberty and democracy….

Which brings us to the reality of today and our future against our long-term enemies, Communists, Socialists, progressive radicals and most of all in these dangerous times, deadly Islamic terrorists who are determined to rule the world at all costs – primarily the destruction of the United States of America and the free world. Unfortunately, we are being blindly undermined by the enemy within….

And there lies the crossroads of America's survival – the ruinous, un-American Democrat Party, propelled into power by the gross mistake of Barrack Obama, and our insidious news media Mafia who know not what they do, against all of us, them included… It has been a destructive exercise in futility!

Fortunately, God is good, and gave us President Donald Trump and a Republican Congress instead of Hillary Clinton. Indeed, instead of Doom – Deliverance!

Daniel B. Jeffs

President Obama vs. America
(Round 7 starts with a $4 trillion budget)

In the deadly hostile environment of ISIS, al-Qaeda and Taliban terrorists, it has become painfully clear that President Obama is covering his arrogant ineptness and refusal to deal with the imminent dangers to our national security by insulting the intelligence of the American people.

Indeed, since when did Taliban terrorists -- controlling Afghanistan and joining with Osama bin-Laden's al-Qaeda to plot and carry out the 9/11 attacks on America -- become *insurgents*?

The answer is simple: Since the president traded 5 top level Taliban terrorists for Army Sgt. Bowe Bergdahl, an American deserter and traitor who collaborated with the Taliban for 5 years, costing the lives of 5 of our troops searching for him. Since President Obama surrendered Iraq, Syria, Afghanistan and Middle East to Iran and the radical Islamic Jihad against all non-conforming Muslims, Israel, America and the West.

Surely, Mr. Obama's Taliban prisoner exchange intentions were to appease the Taliban – followed by closing Guantanamo and giving it back to Cuba -- suppress Bergdahl's military prosecution and quietly slip him out of the military with a dishonorable discharge – not to mention ignoring the ongoing Taliban terrorist takeover of nuclear Pakistan, recently costing the lives of 132 school children.

President Obama is the antithesis of a responsible U.S. President and Commander-in-Chief, and he is betraying the American people with his dangerous ineptness, distractions, deceptions, lies, abuse of power machinations and parsing official language – too numerous to include here -- in the blind pursuit of his un-American agenda

Unfortunately, impeachment is not an option for the first black president. Hopefully, with an $18 trillion national debt, and coming out with a $4 trillion budget in Round 7, America can survive the sucker-punches of Mr. Obama's last two years in office. And hopefully, wised-up voters, a reformed media and a Republican president and

Congress can undo what Obama/Democrats have wrought upon our society and lead us out of the liberal wilderness to the light of freedom and recovery.

President Obama is waging war against coal, oil and much more

President Obama and his liberal Democrat culture have been waging war against America since his 2008 election. Clearly, the president's latest attack against oil by designating 1.5 million oil-rich acres in Alaska a wilderness area, and refusal to approve the Keystone Pipeline -- added to his EPA's crushing blows against the coal industry -- is painful proof of his campaign promise that our electric bills would necessarily "skyrocket," in favor of costly and unreliable renewable energy.

Indeed, we now know that when then Senator Obama boldly stated that he was going to fundamentally transform America -- by undermining our security and freedoms with extreme social, political and economic divisions -- he meant it.

Certainly, President Obama and his Democrat Congress undermined our economic freedoms with his Unaffordable Careless Act, and the Dodd Frank finance legislation. Worse, Mr. Obama's foreign policy and feckless war against terrorism has put our nation at extreme risk, particularly by playing into the feigned negotiating hands of the world's largest state sponsor of terrorism, Iran while they develop nuclear weapons and expand their influence throughout the Middle East – with little or no resistance.

Surely, President Obama blatantly lied in his 2015 State of the Union speech when he said that he had no more campaigns to run, when in fact he has never stopped campaigning, and won't stop during his last two years in office. The question is, how much more damage will he inflict upon us? Fortunately, Congress is now controlled by Republicans, albeit subject to Mr. Obama's veto. Hopefully, the presidency will go to a Republican in 2016 instead of incompetent Hillary Clinton – a poor choice for the first woman president – as it sadly was for the first black president.

Alas, America is steeped in uncertainty from being assaulted by big government, abuse of power, regulations taxation and debt – and battered by the failures of good intentions. Hopefully, the Republican

Party will nominate Wisconsin Governor Scott Walker, with an articulate running-mate such as Sen. Rubio or Gov. Huckabee. Governor Walker is an honest man with high integrity, state executive experience, and he will be strong for our society, our economy and our national security.

Clearly, our freedoms, our future, our security and democracy are in the hands of our fellow voters – a voter nation of fools -- until we took control of the House in 2010, slipped back to President Obama in 2012 – then took control of the Senate in 2014. We will need someone like Governor Walker in 2016, to pick up the pieces of our unique republic, recover and move on to true liberty real democracy and prosperity.

Daniel B. Jeffs

Acknowledgements

I wish to thank and acknowledge all of the newspapers and news-magazines that published my letters to the editor.

In terms of television news, I would like to extend my appreciation to *NewsCorp* and the *Fox News Channel* for providing fair and balanced truth in reporting the news.

In stark contrast to what is disturbingly disseminated by the biased news cartel of *ABC, CBS, NBC, CNN and MSNBC* and most major print news media. Unfortunately, what had become known as America's national newspaper, *USA TODAY* has taken a hard political left turn -- along with what is supposed to be the completely objective *Associated Press.*

Fortunately, print media such as the *Wall Street Journal, New York Post,* the *Washington Times, Washington Examiner* and *Freedom Communications* print media practice responsible journalism.

And I must echo the sentiment, "Thank you *C-Span*" for their neutral, uncut coverage of politics, government, social and economic policy without editorials. An additional thank you goes to *C-Span* for providing unparalleled public access to telephone and email democracy. Real democracy is being practiced at *C-Span.*

Of course, there is a great appreciation to information and communications technology industry, and the purveyors of the Internet for dramatically expanding the voice of the people, democracy, freedom of expression and the resources for limitless information.

However, I am deeply concerned about the dark side of the rapidly advancing social media era, and much worse, the ominous side of fake internet news, cyber crime and terrorism that affects our politics, economics, society and national security.

CONTENTS

AND INDEX TO PUBLISHED LETTERS

2015 Letters

FOREWORD

We have it in our power to begin the world over again.

— Thomas Paine
Common Sense

The only thing necessary for evil to exist is for good people to remain silent.

— Edmund Burke
(paraphrased)

America is steeped in uncertainty. Our society has been relentlessly assaulted by selfish interests and battered by the failures of good intentions. The time to save our democracy is now.

— Daniel B. Jeffs
America's Crisis

Our nation has been unduly influenced by a superficial society of socialist aggression, political chaos, selfish interests and extremes. We must hold on to our liberty, and keep a tight grip on our freedom.

The shame of good deeds is they are not appreciated for generations. The tragedy of bad deeds is they are not resisted until it's too late.

— Daniel B. Jeffs
Letters to the Editor

INTRODUCTION

It has been profoundly said, and how true it is, that the only thing necessary for evil to exist is for good people to remain silent. — Edmund Burke (paraphrased)

Sometime during most people's lives they have either written or had the urge to write a letter to the editor of their newspaper. The event is usually brought on by something they perceive as good or bad that happened in their community, their state or the nation. People are often stimulated by strong feelings about something they have personally experienced, seen on television or read in the newspaper.

Unfortunately, most people's letters don't get published. The main reason is that newspapers simply receive too many letters to publish them all. Other reasons range from rambling, lengthy letters, to angry letters that are too inflammatory, or letters that simply don't make sense.

Most editors prefer concise letters, limited to between 150 and 300 words, which they can tie-in or "tag" to "hot-button" issues covered by their newspapers.

Over twenty years ago I began to write letters about issues I felt strongly about. I achieved some success with letters published in my local and regional newspapers. As I learned the language and the types of comments on issues that editors were looking for, my letters improved. Then I began submitting letters to national newspapers and newsmagazines, many of which were published. Letters from others with differing views on a particular issue have been included where possible.

This book contains helpful tips on writing letters and the 16 of the author's published letters commenting on major national, state and local news events and issues over the past 2 years, with emphasis on the abuse of power by President Obama and the 2016 presidential election. Together with Volumes 1, 2, 3, 4 and 5 of his work covering the previous 20 years, the author has 687 published letters. Volume 3 contains the author's unpublished letters (2007-2011). Volumes 4, 5 and 6 include unpublished letters.

One objective of this book is to help you write letters to the editor that will have a better chance at being published. In addition to suggestions for writing letters to the editor, I have included a few tips on writing other effective letters. After all, most of us would like to be heard from down here in the trenches of democracy and we need all the help we can get.

Regardless of your views, as you read through the book, it should assist you in creating issues, arguing issues and to develop your own commentary and letter-writing style. Learn the media's language, be concise, keep writing and your voice will be heard.

We must never underestimate the power of our words. Unless we break your silence, support what we believe in and speak out against tyranny and injustice, we cannot expect to hold on to our liberty.

The September 11, 2001 attack on America and the war against terrorism abruptly changed our lives. Terrorist attacks against us around the world continue, and we remain under the threat of another terrorist attack on our homeland -- possibly a nuclear attack.

The 2008 economic collapse, the election of Barack Obama as president, and the Democrat-controlled Congress seriously diminished our individual liberties and freedoms, and reduced our national security. Now, more than ever, we must be aware of what is going on in our society, our government and around the world. We should educate ourselves, ask questions and demand answers. Writing letters to the editor is an accessible way to do it, and one of the most valuable tools of free speech.

It's time for the silent majority of middle-America to speak out, as is being done with the spontaneous Tea Party movement reacting to the over-reaching expansion, regulation, taxation and control by government. Fortunately, the Tea Party movement resulted in

Republicans taking control of the House of Representative, and gaining seats in the Senate in 2010.

Unfortunately, President Obama was re-elected, Democrats gained more seats in the Senate, and the Republican House is the only thing keeping us from being consumed by forces beyond our control and losing our democracy. Fortunately, Republicans gained control of the Senate in 2014, and their seats in the House. President Obama is now at war against the Republican Congress and our economy, but neglecting our national security and failing in the war against terrorism.

Hopefully, Republicans will win the presidency in 2016 and restore our democracy.

Meanwhile, the expansion of the Internet, communications technology, and new media has extended a wealth of information and potential power to all the people. We must use and protect it or lose it to government control and/or cyber attacks from our enemies.

I have spoken out many times on social, political and economic issues and I will continue to do so as long as I am able. I simply cannot leave my family, my community, my state and my country with anything less…

TRIBUTE TO MY SON

Dick Armey's Freedom Works organization conducted a 2009 "I am and Entrepreneur" essay contest in which my submission was one of the winners.

Following is my submission:
http://www.freedomworks.org/content/my-son-is-an-entrepreneur

My son is an Entrepreneur
By Daniel B. Jeffs
Apple Valley, CA
March 7, 2009

My son, John T. Jeffs (nick name: "Jay") is a 42-year-old self-made entrepreneur and innovator. And, of course, I couldn't be prouder of him. Jay is a great man, married with a daughter. He is too modest and humble to tell his own unique story, so I will.

Before I begin, It should be noted that against all odds, Jay built his small business from nothing, in Apple Valley, CA, the town where he lives, employing local people and providing the important products of security mail handling equipment. Of course, his constant challenge has been surviving the unyielding anti-business environment of extreme taxation and regulations by California government. A remarkable accomplishment.

Children are often asked, "What do you want to be when you grow up?" While Jay was excavating a project in the dirt yard with his Tonka trucks, I asked him the question. He replied, "I'm gonna be a workin' man." And that's what he became. While growing up he wanted to work with me around the house and yard, making improvements and working on the car. He loved to work with tools and to make things. In junior high school woodshop, he made an amazing laminated cutting board for his mother from various hardwoods. She still uses it today.

Jay's work ethic was established early. He helped the family when times were tough, skipped high school sports so he could work after school and contribute his paycheck, and he never complained. His first job was working at a local pizza parlor, then for a new Carl's Jr. in town, where he worked his way up to assistant manager. Then we worked for the Old Quaker Paint Company, saved his money, and bought into a quick-lube business. Soon after, he joined a credit union and established his first credit with a small loan.

But Jay wasn't satisfied with working for others. He wanted to start his own business and be an entrepreneur. While still working at the paint company and quick lube, he decided to do something no one else was doing. Sell, install and repair curbside mailboxes for people. It was 1987, and the U.S. Postal Service was changing to curbside service from mail trucks instead of door to door mail service. The curbside mailbox was the last thing new homeowners installed, which were not included when new homes were built. It was a chore because people had to buy a mailbox, post and house numbers, along with a posthole digger if they didn't have one. Plus, most curbside mailboxes were rural-style, not secure and easily damaged by vandals with bats, or broken by being struck by vehicles.

Jay placed an ad describing his new service in the local newspaper. The basic service was for a box, post and numbers installed for $30.00. At first the response was slow, but when people responded, word-of-mouth increased the business. Jay had a pick-up truck, and he used my hand tools, power tools and posthole digger to do the work. He purchased mailboxes from a distributor and offered several styles and models. Then when tracts of homes were being built in the area, he obtained a contract to install mailboxes, which led to additional contracts. It was less expensive for builders to subcontract with Jay than to use their own carpenters.

It wasn't long before Jay expanded to sales and installations of commercial and residential multiple mailbox units, which he purchased from a dealer in the Los Angeles area. The dealer was also a commercial mail handling equipment contractor who asked Jay to do installations for them because they lost their installer. Jay agreed and expanded his experience to installing equipment in mailrooms, office and apartment buildings, along with mail chutes, bank chutes and laundry chutes in high rise buildings. Subsequently, he obtained his own specialty contractor's license. And he received a timely $3,000 inheritance from a great uncle who sensed something special in Jay as an eager toddler.

While all this was going on, our home became a mailbox business. Jay used the garage for his shop, and the mailboxes were assembled in the house by my wife. He bought a larger truck, more power tools, built several sheds to store product and supplies, and the house was filled with assembled boxes. Then Jay took a bigger step and began bidding on and getting more commercial and larger jobs, including apartments and mobile home parks. It wasn't long before my wife and I had to run away from home. We sold the house to Jay, and bought another home nearby.

With all the experience Jay absorbed, and the fact that mail theft was becoming a significant problem, Jay invented and patented the highest quality security mailbox available and trademarked it as the Letter Locker. After being tested and approved by the Postmaster General, the examiner was so impressed by it that he bought one. Soon, Jay built a large shop behind the house and began manufacturing the Letter Locker. He contracted out the fabrication, welding and powder-coating, and my wife did his office work and helped assemble Letter Lockers along with Jay's first employee. It wasn't long before our new garage was converted to assemble more boxes.

Jay secured more and more dealers for the Letter Locker and continued to expand, including the development of a rear loading model and a Supreme model that could receive and store more mail and larger parcels and packages. Then came the big step. He formed Jayco Industries as a limited liability corporation, and purchased a light industrial building on 15 acres where he manufactured the entire Letter Locker, which became the core of his business. He also became the largest western regional distributor for Auth-Florence mail handling equipment.

The business continued to grow, and by the turn of the century Jay had 85 dealers, 15 employees, 20 various size trucks, state-of-the-art metal manufacturing machinery. He expanded with satellite offices in Las Vegas, San Diego and Denver, and purchased the 15 acres of land next to his plant. When the USPS upgraded mailbox standards, they established security mailbox standards, using the Letter Locker as a model.

Jay recently invented an even more secure locking device for mailboxes, "The Claw Lock," which is available as an upgrade option on Letter Lockers, particularly, the heavy-duty model. He has websites for Letter Lockers and Jayco Industries at: http://www.letterlocker.com and http://www.jaycoindustries.com

Of course, since the economic downturn in the housing market, Jay's business has slowed significantly. He is holding on as best as he can, supported by slower, but steady sales of Letter Lockers, commercial equipment and custom security boxes. Jay is a great employer and boss. He is fair and honest with his employees, who have the utmost respect for him. And he helps them out personally whenever he can. Though he is trying to keep them all employed, he has had to cut back on their hours, and close the Denver office.

Jay became the ideal entrepreneurial success story and he did it on pure self-reliance and hard work. He enjoys an excellent reputation for service in all his business dealings, and with the U.S. Postal Service. Needless to say, we are extremely proud parents, knowing that our son, John T. Jeffs is a well-respected example for anyone to aspire to in our democratic free market society. Indeed, I know of no one, other than my wife and daughter, who work as hard or have as much character and integrity as my son, Jay. For that, my wife and I are very successful family entrepreneurs.

As a footnote, I should add that my wife still assembles Letter Locker flag/bolt kits for the business at our home. And my daughter worked with Jay for a time as his director of operations. I retired in 2006 after working in law enforcement and as an investigator in the criminal justice system for a total of 41 years. I have always done all I could as an American citizen to ensure our continued security, liberty and freedom.

✳ ✳ ✳ ✳

May 11, 2009

Dear Daniel,

Thank you for entering our "I Am an Entrepreneur" competition to help us celebrate the entrepreneur. Congratulations! You are one of our runners-up--great work. We'll be sending your prize in the mail within the next two weeks.

If you'll send along your mailing information to Clark Ruper I'd appreciate it.

If you're interested, we have posted an announcement and links to all the winners on FreedomWorks.org

Thanks again for helping us celebrate the entrepreneur,

Joseph Onorati
Staff Writer
FreedomWorks

ENLIGHTENING
EXPERIENCES

To better understand my writing, a summary of my background might be helpful:

The most enlightening and fulfilling experience of my life has been my wife, Wilma and our children. Wilma and I raised two boys and a girl through the 60's, 70's and into the 80's. I began my life career as a cop in 1960. Wilma was a full-time mother, except during tough financial times. We were high school sweethearts and celebrated our 57th anniversary on July 31, 2016. When asked about the success of our long marriage my answer is, ups and downs notwithstanding, the most important thing is to be best friends. And it always helps to have a good dog as a member of the family.

My better half is undoubtedly the best wife, mother and partner on the planet. She was deeply involved with our children throughout their school years. We witnessed the beginning of the end of education as we knew it. If she hadn't supplemented their education at home, our children would not be the well-rounded people they are today. It took our combined efforts to teach them about character, consideration, discipline, friendship, work ethic, the ways of life, and to guide them through the failing social and political environment closing-in around them, which is something far more difficult for parents to deal with today. It is even more difficult and frustrating for single parents.

I was a deputy sheriff with the Los Angeles County Sheriff's Department from 1960 to 1967. During the first half of the decade the crime we identify with today was minimal. I worked the streets and neighborhoods and there were no significant problems with drugs, drunk-driving, domestic violence, sex crimes, child abuse, or guns and violence among young people. The civil rights movement and riots notwithstanding, there was mutual respect between law enforcement and the general public.

That all began to change when I went to work for the San Bernardino County Sheriff's Department (1967-1980). The social, political and criminal law revolution took hold. Elements of the baby boomer generation rejected their parents – now known as the greatest generation – and the so-called establishment. They launched the drug culture, took over education and, eventually, government. The rest is history, since revised, and I have personally witnessed most of it.

During my 20-year career as a patrolman, detective, sergeant, academy instructor and community college instructor I communicated with and observed people of all ages and from nearly every walk of life. I related to people on the streets, in their homes, where they went to school, where they worked and where the found recreation.

My approach to law enforcement changed when I realized that I didn't have to win every fight. I found it much more productive talking common sense with people and being fair and understanding. I discovered that many people could be helped at that most vulnerable moment in their lives when they crossed paths with a cop. It could be either a negative, often devastating experience, or a helpful learning experience.

The easy way was to carry a ten-pound badge and intimidate people. I found it difficult to work with other cops who acted like that. But it wasn't unusual during that brief period that I call "cop adolescence" when a young officer turns from an insecure rookie into a first-stage veteran. It happens after about 2 years on the job and it happened to me.

It's almost like being that indestructible teenager who knows everything, that is, until the raging hormones settle down and you're blinded by the stark reality that you have to get through the rest of life on your own. Most of us come out of it. Some don't and they're stuck in virtual immaturity. Unfortunately, if that happens to cops, they can be extremely dangerous to society.

Though it was often frowned upon in "cop shops", I established a good reputation with both prosecutors and defense attorneys because I would not seek a criminal complaint against anyone unless the investigation was honest and complete, both from a prosecution standpoint and a defense point of view. In other words, rather than focusing with prosecution blinders, I would resist arresting or trying to convict a person unless I was convinced by a thorough investigation that the person was guilty.

Some of my extraordinary experiences in law enforcement included the emerging reasons behind the Los Angeles Watts Riots of 1965 and working joint jurisdiction with the military at the 29 Palms Marine Corps Base in California during the controversial Vietnam War. My overall enlightening experience was the nation's cultural and political revolution that would lead to my leaving law enforcement in 1980. By then the writing was engraved on the wall.

Thomas Paine was 39 when he took on the passionate cause of freedom from tyranny. Though I don't pretend to be a Thomas Paine, I too was 39 when a similar burning desire first surfaced in me. I had an established career in law enforcement and attained the three-hat position of the sheriff's department personnel, legal and affirmative action officer. While working at headquarters, I was exposed to the dark side of politics in the department and in county government.

It didn't take long for my naive bubble to burst when I discovered that the sheriff wanted me to find a legal way around a recent court decision prohibiting him from summarily firing people without due process. And though I was the affirmation action officer, I was told not to take any affirmative action beyond going through the motions of getting the department off probation. It took even less time for me to realize that the sheriff, known as the "J. Edgar Hoover" of the county, maintained dual personnel files and intelligence files on everyone from city council members to county supervisors and judges. Anyone of power, wealth and influence in the county carried one of his badges.

With some encouragement from others in the department, in 1978 – the year of California's Proposition 13 tax revolt – I ran against my boss. He was a 25-year unopposed county sheriff, who abdicated his responsibility and abandoned our department and the citizens of the county to political infighting among his potential successors. Though unsuccessful, my family and I received a brutal education in dirty reality of political campaigns. My candidacy did, however, cause the sheriff to step down after the term. In time, the effort helped to accomplish many of the needed changes and improvements for the department and the county.

I continued my political education in 1980 by running for county supervisor to improve conditions in my district, which is very large and difficult to represent. My chances of being elected looked promising because I had done well in the district when I ran for sheriff. I campaigned on making county government accountable and more responsive. And I thought about how more democracy might improve representation. However, a wealthy landowner jumped in at the last moment and bought the election. My days of running for public office were over and my family couldn't have been happier.

Since I had been transferred to the county jail as a "political prisoner" just 3 days after announcing my candidacy for sheriff, my days in law enforcement were also over. I resigned shortly after losing the supervisor election. It was time for me to get out anyway. Sheriffs and police chiefs had far too much political power. Law enforcement dynasties were corrupt. And the new breed of young cops was disturbing. Too many of them were the first products of an aggressive, irresponsible generation.

Gross conflicts of interest caught up with the land baron who bought the 1980 supervisor's election. He was recalled after two years in office. Though I vowed never to run for office again, I did assist the recall candidate who succeeded him by writing a campaign platform that was responsible for getting him elected.

Voters were encouraged by the campaign platform because it was based upon a form of direct democracy for the candidate's constituents. The idea was to have citizen advisory councils comprised of members from every element of each community, selected by the people from those elements, not political appointees.

The Community Council concept was designed to give some direction to the supervisor as their representative and to provide a conduit for him to keep communities in the district informed about county government, including a complete accounting of their tax dollars. In addition, the council concept would provide the elements of each community with a communications medium to better understand each other's problems and concerns, and the ability to establish their priorities.

Unfortunately, like most people who become politicians, the supervisor was seduced by county politics, bureaucrats and his new-found personal power. Under pressure from the communities, he reluctantly formed several community councils. But after his election to a full term he made it painfully clear that he didn't want to be told what to do by the people in his district. The supervisor was soundly defeated in his bid for re-election. And the frustrating cycle of failures in representation continued. Fortunately, the current supervisor is competent young man who seems to grasp what it takes to do a good job.

After working for several years as the lead dispatcher for a joint powers communications center serving 5 fire departments, I learned how well city, county, state and federal fire agencies could work together, something rare among law enforcement agencies and departments. I also gained an education in city government and politics.

Then in 1985 I returned to work for San Bernardino County as a public defender investigator. While in law enforcement I earned a law degree so that I would know as much as lawyers in the system. But I did not go on to become a practicing attorney because I was simply incompatible with lawyers and their closed, questionable legal communities that were growing less and less desirable for someone like me.

The one thing that I learned from the law enforcement and legal professions was that they are both "closed communities." Law enforcement is closed within what could be called the "brotherhood of cops" because they are conditioned not to trust anyone but their own. The legal profession is a loosely knit brotherhood haunted by the constant conflict between doing the right thing and the "what's in it for me?" syndrome.

I have no problem working with lawyers in the criminal justice system. They are good, dedicated people and they have a tough, demanding job to do. I worked well with prosecutors and now defense attorneys, but I simply could not be one of them, rigidly confined to a cumbersome court system. Yet I had come full circle. I retired. And through it all, I've always maintained a particular interest in constitutional law.

The fire of democracy was rekindled in me in early 1991. I began watching politics and government on a larger scale and realized how dangerously our system had eroded. I wondered how the people could possibly bring about change in government so large, so remote, yet so entrenched in our lives. While writing *Black Robes on White Horses,"* a novel about the Supreme Court gaining too much power, I came up with the idea of direct democracy voting networks connected to voters' homes as the solution to runaway government. It had to be something more than merely responding to manipulated elections with predictable results.

Later that year, under the pseudonym of John Citizen, I took a giant leap by writing a small pamphlet proposing an amendment to the Constitution that would establish direct democracy. The proposal would enable citizens to control of government with direct democracy. It would establish a genuine government by the people.

The proposed 28th Amendment was intended to update and fix the Constitution and to provide voters with a method of communications to better understand each other's problems, concerns and priorities.

Then the presidential election year of 1992 rolled-in on the back of a recession. The opposing players were type-cast the same as the 1980 election when Ronald Reagan took the presidency away from recession-plagued Jimmy Carter. This time, however, they're roles would be reversed, not because of the recession, but because of a bee in the ointment that would turn into a political swarm.

Ross Perot buzzed onto the scene with an appearance on CNN's Larry King Live. Perot caught the people's attention with his billionaire status and his proposition that "The people are the owners of the country." The corny little guy touched a national nerve and created an overnight sensation when he promised that, if the people put him on the ballot in all 50 states, he would put on a "world class" campaign and help them take back the country from a government in default.

All the political pundits were confused, uneasy and often unnerved from the phenomenal public response to Perot and his call for volunteers to take up their voting arms. I was encouraged by his direct democracy concept of an "Electronic Town Hall" laser-beamed to the White House so the people could give him direction as their servant.

I was more impressed by the spontaneous national response to a figure of hope. People actually got out and participated in democracy by getting Perot on the ballot in all 50 states. Charged with enthusiasm, I re-directed my efforts to sending Perot a flow of information about the 28th Amendment and voting networks that would truly put all political power in the hands of the people.

But I got absolutely no response other than an indirect offer to be a volunteer. In the end, Perot served only to frustrate and confuse his devoted volunteers. He betrayed the people by his in-and-out and then back-in candidacy for president, his deceitful personal agenda and his hunger to be "King of America."

Two months before Election Day, I published and distributed the proposed 28th Amendment pamphlet. I sent copies to all the candidates for president, the leaders of Congress, the governors and legislatures of every state and the mainstream press.

During those efforts I didn't know much about Thomas Paine and the vital part he played the American Revolution. I didn't know about his writing and the publishing of *Common Sense*. I didn't know that Paine first wrote his pamphlet under the name of *an Englishman,* and had it published at his own expense.

1992 was an election year of unusual discontent and I was certain the idea of the 28th Amendment would surface, somewhere, somehow. But there was no response from anyone. Even my own Congressman did not reply until I confronted him with a personal letter. His response was a pat on the head, while condescending to me that it was a "novel idea." I was even more astonished by the eerie silence of the media, then I realized they simply don't pay any attention to common people unless there's something outrageous or zoo-like attached to it. Something for them to feed upon.

Perot left us with a legacy that he and we would come to regret. Arkansas Governor Bill Clinton slipped into the presidency. Perot could not abide the dark side of politics coming at him. When he perceived that President Bush and his campaign for re-election were playing dirty, he threw enough support to Bill Clinton to hand him the election with only 43 percent of the vote.

In an election as important as the presidency of the United States, no one should be elected to that office with less than a 50 percent plus one vote majority. If there hadn't been a 12th Amendment and the Electoral College there would have and should have been a run-off election. The 12th Amendment should have been repealed long ago. The election of the president should be by popular vote, and the matter should have been included in the 17th Amendment when the election of U.S. senators was changed to popular vote in 1913.

Ross Perot did, however, play an unwitting role in stimulating an effort to complete the American Revolution. He opened a door for the people to organize, exercise democracy and be heard in the political process of voicing their opinions about public policy. It cost Perot millions to open that door, but he slammed it shut with his inconsistent moods and his obsessions for domination and control. Somehow, Perot reminded me of that supervisor who was all for democracy until it came to yielding his power.

Nevertheless, like the few communities in my district, millions of voters tasted real democracy, if only for a brief time. The question remaining was, would it serve as a lasting passion for self-government? In the aftermath, Perot left his volunteers with the organization of United We Stand America to influence candidates, elections and public policy. The National Patriot Party was formed from other elements of his volunteers. Then Perot formed the Reform Party and ran again in 1996, but the people had lost interest in the little fraud with a big mouth.

We cannot overlook another powerful indicator of a rooting revolution. Rush Limbaugh. His booming radio voice has fired-up the minds of what millions of people are thinking. Limbaugh has become a monument to the conservative Republican agenda and a daily reminder of the evils inherent in the big liberal government of Democrats and the liberal mainstream press.

Limbaugh's success spawned a multitude of conservative hosts in the rising power of talk radio.

Like Perot, Limbaugh's philosophy was powerfully inviting. Also like Perot, I sent Limbaugh information about the 28th Amendment and the people's voting network, with no response. Neither Perot, Limbaugh, nor anyone with real power would be willing to give it up to the people, including the national media.

Sadly, I realized that the media was hardened by the lust for rating dollars and status. They were obsessed with elite politics and celebrities, real, created or imagined, simply because it sells. Their corporate owners abandoned their responsibilities under the privileges of the First Amendment for the sake of profits. The media just wasn't concerned about the public interest in freedom and democracy, only its own liberal agenda. It's no wonder our citizens feel so helpless, disenfranchised and alone.

Knowing that California had always been on the cutting edge of political revolution, I began looking into an effort to place a constitutional initiative on the ballot that would establish direct democracy with a secure electronic voting network. I thought, if direct democracy could be established in California, other states would follow.

While studying the California Constitution, I was drawn to Article II. *Voting, Initiative and Referendum, and Recall.* Curiously, Section 1 [Purpose of Government] declares that "All political power is inherent in the people. Government is instituted for their protection, security and benefit, and they have the right to alter or reform it when the public good may require." Sounds good. Just like a democratic republic.

But it doesn't work that way. I soon realized the California Constitution was extremely complex. Ballot initiatives and referendums were not designed for the people because the process is too costly, restrictive and self-defeating for most citizens even to attempt. Rather, it's dominated by powerful moneyed special interests and the legislature. They play with people's minds and sell them out with deceitful ballot measures. Whenever a real people's initiative does pass, it is often circumvented by government, litigated against by special interests, or invalidated by the courts.

Depressed by the realization that so many people had lost the will to think about the true circumstances in which they live, I found it difficult to understand how people had become conditioned to selfish interests and dependency. How they'd come to expect government to fix everything. And how marginalized democracy was.

It took me a while to regain my determination and to renew my efforts to get the message out. During the California ballot initiative attempt, I solicited support from taxpayer and public interest groups such as the Howard Jarvis and Gann organizations of California Proposition 13 tax revolt fame that spread across the country. They were intrigued by the idea, however, they declined to assist because they had limited resources committed to specialized tax-related efforts. I sensed they wished it could happen, but there was a bitter flavor of futility in their responses.

Understandably, partisan politics, big government and large corporate interests including the media have reason to fear the idea of direct democracy. It would be terrifying for them to know that they could lose control of the country to the people. After all, they do have vested interests in choking off the voice of the people, keeping us ignorant, mute and conditioned to accept being insignificant.

I was so caught-up in the passions of my convictions that I didn't know how deeply low-esteem had been ingrained in the minds of the people. When acquaintances read the idea they agreed with the concept, but conceded that "They," meaning corporate and government power, would never let it happen.

Some displayed their lack of confidence in the people accepting the responsibility of direct democracy. Others felt that the public was too ignorant and irresponsible to handle it. Though their responses were discouraging I sensed a spark in their eyes telling me that they hoped for it to happen.

When I explained to them that their doubts were understood because there has been no credible experience with direct democracy since the birth of democracy in Athens, Greece 2500 years ago. And when I told them about the political power over taxation and public policy they could have at their fingertips, nearly all of them felt a sense of urgency for direct democracy.

In my first attempt to circulate a proposed 28th Amendment, I detailed everything I could think of about revising the Constitution. Since then, I've condensed and simplified the proposal, which included a proposal for direct education because I felt it was nearly as important to our future as direct democracy. I thought anyone could easily conclude that computers, telecommunications and information technology would dominate our future. The question remained, would we control it or would it control us? It was time to decide. Our future would depend on it.

It was also time for me to make a decision. Encouraged by my daughter, I gave up my typewriter and bought my first computer with a word processor. But how could I write on a computer? It was so complicated and distracting, how could I concentrate? Now, I can't imagine how I wrote so much on a typewriter or ever going back to using one. From that point on, I became a social, economic, technology, education and political observer, determined to speak out against our declining society and in favor of a better America. And, of course, I established a Website to promote direct democracy – something most people in power fear, for fear of losing power.

THE STRUGGLE TO BE HEARD

The failure of the two-party system and the 1992 Ross Perot candidacy for president caused me to change my voter registration from Republican to nonpartisan independent. I was a moderate, detested by leftwing liberals such as Ted Kennedy and rightwing conservatives such as Rush Limbaugh who believe that moderates stand for nothing. But, along with millions of other moderates who participated in democracy to get Perot elected, I became a passionate moderate determined to be heard.

Frustration filled my mind as I stared at the blank page in front of me. It was 1993 and I felt a deep sense of betrayal. Ross Perot handed the election to Bill Clinton out of spite for President Bush. I lost all the equity in my home, and it was worth less than my mortgage because of the recession and a steep decline in the real estate market. The American people seemed to have lost the will to fight for the kind of real democracy promised by Perot, and I was about to write my first letter to the editor of our local newspaper to vent my anger. I have since forgotten what it was about.

Anyway, I wrote the letter and sent it off in the mail. I kept writing letters to my local and regional newspapers, but couldn't seem to get any of them published. Then I began to read other people's letters, hoping to get a feel for the content of letters that had the best chance of making it to the printed page. Still, my letters got no response from the editors.

Soon I realized that published letters to the editor were not as hostile as mine, and they were writing about things they read in the newspaper, including other people's letters. So I took a lesson from that and finally got a letter or two published. When my regional newspaper, The San Bernardino Sun, published a commentary that I submitted to a column called, "It's Your Turn," I finally felt that I was on my way to being heard.

While writing my first novel, I was told to write about what I know. I had a brutal education about politics and government. I knew about the criminal justice system. And I experienced the troubling failure of public education and the disturbing decline of society. So I began to write letters about current events that I knew about and other things I was concerned about. I also learned that editors responded to letters that grabbed their attention, beginning and ending with "hook" sentences, which was a little something I picked up from lessons on creative writing.

In 1995, I decided to expand my letter writing to larger audiences, so I began writing letters to major newspapers and newsmagazines. It took a while, but on August 31, 1995, USA TODAY published my letter about the information technology revolution and direct democracy. I was further encouraged when USA TODAY published another letter about home education on September 19, 1995, and yet another letter about education in December. It was like a shot of adrenaline to me when America's only national newspaper published my letters. However, it was short-lived and I wouldn't get another letter published for over a year.

Meanwhile, I kept the letters going. My local and regional newspapers published many of them, and I was gaining somewhat of a reputation for speaking out about things other people were thinking strongly about. My friends, family, co-workers and many other people I knew agreed with my letters and brought it to my attention when they hadn't seen one lately because they looked forward to reading them.

By 1996, I had one letter published in TIME magazine, two in the Washington Times, and one in the Los Angeles Times. Then I decided to go for what I called a "Grand Slam" of published letters. At least one letter published in the five top print media: USA TODAY, The New York Times, The Washington Post, The Los Angeles Times and TIME Magazine. I had achieved three out of five. The New York Times and The Washington Post would prove to be the most difficult. Eventually, I would make the grand slam several times over.

Though I'm not a highly skilled writer, I found that ordinary people understood and responded to plain language rather than condescending, intellectual drivel. I also found that my increasing success in getting letters published would be the result of improving my writing by writing as often and as much as I could. And I found it interesting that New York Times and Washington Post editors would not publish a letter from a "commoner" unless it was very brief and edited by them.

It wasn't until 1998 that I got a letter published in the Washington Post, which was about John Glenn going back in space. Then in 1999, the grand slam was complete with a letter published in the New York Times and another in the Washington Post. The Washington Times – the other Washington newspaper – began publishing more and more of my letters, and it seemed as though I was their West Coast correspondent. That is, until they cut me off when the 2000 presidential elections rolled around, the stock market and the economy went sour, and I was writing too much about democracy and against the two-party system.

However, USA TODAY picked up on many of my letters and published them through the remainder of 1999, all of 2000 and the presidential election farce, and into 2001. Those were good letter-writing years. Several more were published in the Los Angeles Times, TIME Magazine and U.S. News & World Report. Of course I was still getting letters published in my local and regional newspapers.

After the September 11, 2001 attack on America, the competition to be heard was fierce. Everything changed. People and society, even government and politics seemed to change for the better, at least for a while. But the encouraging trend wouldn't last. After the stock market bubble burst – and the distraction of the retaliatory War in Afghanistan was over – corporate corruption was exposed and politics as usual reared its ugly head again during the 2002 elections. Then again over the controversial war in Iraq, and into the 2004 presidential election cycle, the social and political war games were well underway...

The struggle to be heard is an endless, particularly for the vast majority of people in every city, county and state in America. Most people are too busy working, raising families and trying to survive in a stressed-out society steeped in uncertainty. Too many people are resigned to believing they can't do anything to change things when they see something wrong. But this is a new era of information technology. Learn to write well enough to express your views and ideas simply and concisely, and you will be heard. If not in the newspaper, you can express yourself by writing letters to television news programs, radio programs or over the Internet in chat rooms, blog sites and to the expanding new media.

The information technology revolution and the age of new media have extended the opportunity for many more people to express themselves. Even television news programming has caught on to asking for and publishing more and more of people's letters – *The Fox News Channel* and Bill O'Reilly's "folks," for example. O'Reilly published a total of four of my e-mails and commented on them.

My first nonfiction book, *America's Crisis: The Direct Democracy and Direct Education Solution* was published in September 2000. It was featured on *C-Span BookTV* in early 2001. Some of the positive feedback I received was about the 25 letters to the editor I included at the end of the book, thus, the idea for writing and compiling the first letters to the editor book. *Letters to the Editor: From the Trenches of Democracy* published in 2005 was written for a large audience of moderate independents, squeezed uncomfortably between liberals and conservatives, who feel disenfranchised with little to no voice or power. That is, until it comes to being a consumer of goods and politics. And we all know that those in power are either trying to sell us something we don't need or to make money or to pander to us with lies and deceit to get elected or to stay in office. I felt the first letters book could help turn that around on them. Published or not, editors take serious note of what people have to say in their letters.

I retired in 2006, after a total of 41 years working in the criminal justice system. I served for 7 years with the Los Angeles County Sheriff's Department, 13 years with the San Bernardino County Sheriff's Department, and 21 years as a San Bernardino County Public Defender Investigator. After retiring, I served as a member of the 2007-2008 San Bernardino County Grand Jury -- and again in 2010-2011 -- which was an even more enlightening experience, delving into public corruption within county government. After my service on the Grand Jury, which resulted in the prosecution of the county assessor, a developer, a city councilman and others, I began compiling Volume 2 of Letters to the Editor.

After Volume 2 was published, I compiled my unpublished letters to the editor into Volume 3, after which Volume 4 and 5 were published and I began compiling Volume 6.

THE MEDIA CENSORS IMPORTANT
LETTERS THAT DON'T FIT ITS CULTURE

I have been fortunate to have a number of letters published in major newspapers and news magazines -- such as USA TODAY, The New York Times, Washington Post, Washington Times, Washington Examiner, Los Angeles Times, San Diego Union-Tribune, San Francisco Chronicle, Time Magazine and US News & World Report -- regarding a variety of social, political and economic issues or events.

However, to get my letters published I have had to restrict my comments to current media sensations, acceptable tie-ins to news reports, editorials or commentary, and to limit my criticism to that which fits the media's ideology. Indeed, when it comes to the importance of pointing out the damage extreme feminism has done to relationships, families, men, women and children; or commenting on the divisiveness, hate and discontent perpetuated by the selfish interests of racial activists and the diversity culture; or condemning the academic establishment for robbing generations of students of their education; or criticizing the media culture, which suffers from the unintended consequences of cloaking itself in bias – such letters and the needed balance of views and dialogue from people outside the culture's parochial parameters are deemed politically incorrect, heavily edited, censored or simply ignored.

Unfortunately, with few exceptions, television news media are worse, even more condescending and detached from reality, and they don't or won't share people's feedback unless it fits into their way of thinking (*C-Span* not included). Any doubts were dispelled when I witnessed *New York Times* columnist Maureen Dowd's snide and awkward comparisons of President Bush and Tom Brokaw at the National Press Club's 2003 Fourth Estate Award dinner for the *NBC Nightly News* anchor (held 11-19-03 and subsequently aired on *C-Span*). Dowd's veiled attempt at humor seemingly entertained the media elite in attendance, but she was typically arrogant and about as subtle and satirical as political train-wrecks, Al Franken and Michael Moore.

Most people are informed about what's supposedly going on around them by what they read, see and hear from the major news media. Yet it's troubling to know how reticent the media is about impartial objectivity. And it's troubling to know that many important issues and events are intentionally under-reported or unaddressed, and that most people are unapprised of vital information. It's even more troubling that freedom of the press is a constitutional guarantee, and the media vigorously defends that right, yet they (often unwittingly) censor the very people they are supposed to watch out for and defend. I guess CBS whistleblower (author of *Bias: How the Media Distort the News*) Bernard Goldberg is correct, and that's highly disturbing.

Certainly, glaring examples of bias and censorship have been manifested by media's partisan coverage of the war against terrorism since the September 11, 2001 attack on America and, currently, the war in Iraq. It's frightening to observe how the media consistently attacked President Bush and his administration with anti-war themes, negative reporting and undermining the morale of the military and the people, while failing to report and call former president Clinton and his administration to account for his lack of action against terrorism leading to the attack on America. Surely, our security and our future – and the betrayal of democracy, education and the core of America's culture – is the heavy price society is already paying...

As if the attack on America and the war against terrorism wasn't enough for the nation to endure, the Democrat takeover of Congress in 2006, and the 2008 election of Barack Obama as president, while finance, housing and the economy were imploding, would prove even more disastrous. Though President Bush pushed for reforming Fannie Mae and Freddie Mac, Congress resisted and it was too little, too late.

The root of the crash was forced affordable housing that began with the Carter administration's Community Reinvestment Act. Which was used by the Clinton administration to intimidate banks and mortgage lenders to lower their standards and give home loans to those who could not afford them. Unaffordable housing expanded rapidly throughout the government-backed mortgage securities and finance industry until the bubble burst.

Of course, the collapsing economy, job losses, home foreclosures and bankruptcies were exacerbated by President Obama and the Democrat-controlled Congress passing a wasted $800 billion stimulus bill, national health careless laws, finance regulations and $7 trillion in deficit spending, sending the national debt soaring to over $18 trillion, and pushing us to the fiscal cliff of insolvency.

Alas, none of it will matter if Mr. Obama's abdication of his national security responsibilities, surrendering to the proliferation of the Islamic terrorism of ISIS, al-Qaeda, Iran's expansion and nuclear threat result in all out attacks on Israel, America and the West.

Oops! Now, even though this one was a little hostile and much too long, my letters might be blacklisted. But at least I got it off my chest. Hopefully, my published and unpublished letters will help explain my take on the social, political, economic and national security issues over the past 20 years. Hopefully, the following tips on letter writing will help you express your views, whatever they may be....

TIPS ON LETTER WRITING

Letters to the editor are unique to the newspaper and newsmagazine business. Our history of letters to the editor in the United States date back to the American Revolution. Indeed, the Federalist and Anti-Federalist Papers consisted of letters to the editor from several of our Founders during the constitutional debates.

Newspapers generally use letters to the editor as a public forum for reader reaction to published information on current events. Letters regarding issues that interest opinion and editorial page (Op-Ed) editors are most likely to be published, and that happens to be the first lesson on letter writing.

PICK AN ISSUE

Read editorials and letters to the editor in your newspaper to give you a feel for what editors are looking for. Use other people's letters as a guide to how they approach issues. Editors prefer to see a reference to something in their newspapers. If a letter writer does not refer to an editorial, previous article, commentary or letter, the editor will usually include a reference to the issue.

If an event published in the newspaper grabs your interest or an issue stirs your concerns, that is what you should write about. However, don't write when you are angry. Believe me, it seldom comes out convincing or readable.

Published reports, articles and commentary on issues or events of the day or the week are what editors focus on. Therefore, well-composed letters about major issues and events stand the best chance of being published.

Only a few letters make it past the "tie-in" or "tag" test to stand alone. My unusual "State of the Union" letter published in USA TODAY on September 17, 1997 is one such letter.

Pick a side

If an issue or event is the subject of public debate in the media and you feel strongly about it, one way or the other, pick a side and write a letter. You will stand a better chance of your letter being published if you add something fresh and different to the debate that will interest editors and readers. Sometimes that fresh difference stems from an opinion from the center of an important issue or event.

Letters from the center

Published social, political and economic letters to the editor are dominated by letter writers from the left and right with liberal or conservative bias, even though most people's viewpoints come from the center. In other words, the majority of Americans are moderate centrists.

However, people from the center write fewer letters to editor simply because they are the least active in voicing their opinions about social, political and economic events and issues. On some issues they lean to the left and on other issues they lean to the right. Most centrists identify themselves as leaning socially liberal and fiscally conservative.

I happen to be an independent, moderate centrist who is politically and socially active. Unfortunately, people like me are somewhat rare because of the very nature of moderate label. Actually, I could be described as a "radical" moderate. Contrary to the way it sounds, it is not an oxymoron.

Nevertheless, my centrist approach to writing letters to the editor has contributed to my success in getting letters published, not because the letters are so well written, but because fewer letters from centrists are received by editors and that makes them fresh and different.

HOWEVER

Since Democrats took over the Congress, the economic crash, and the election of Barack Obama, there has been a new awakening in America, including me. When the economic pain hits home, people re-evaluate themselves. Now I, along with the majority of Americans, consider ourselves socially and politically center-right. And as the pain increases, we are moving further to the conservative side.

Bill O'Reilly is a perfect example of a center-right independent. He and Fox News offered the fair and balanced truth in news, and there is a new sheriff in town.

The 2010 mid-term elections proved that by Republicans taking over the House, with gains in the Senate, and throughout state governments. What we need next is control of the Senate and another Ronald Reagan in the White House. A tall order since Reagan was an American original – one of the kind….

That order could have been filled by Mitt Romney and Rep. Paul Ryan in the 2012 presidential election, but with liberal press continuing to back President Obama, he was re-elected.

Learn from journalists

Read articles that interest you, which are written by staff reporters, and examine how they construct their writing. Do the same with Associated Press (AP) articles that have an AP reporter's by-line. Finally, review how editorial writers and columnists present their writing. You can learn from professionals by paying particular attention to the way they begin and end each paragraph.

Begin and end with a "hook"

If you want to catch an editor's eye, you should begin your letter with a hook and end it with a hook. State the problem and offer a solution or conclusion that is likely to grab the editor's interest. The reasons are obvious. Neither editors nor readers will read uninteresting letters.

Likewise, you should begin and end each paragraph in the body of the letter with hook sentences, especially if you want to get a longer letter published. Below are examples of hooks about the "energy crisis" issue:

First sentence hook:
The energy crisis should not have happened, but it did, and we've got government's lack of sound energy policy and corporate greed to thank for it.

Last sentence hook:
Maybe it's time for the people to own and operate "public utilities."

Keep it simple, concise and to the point – "pithy"

Most newspapers limit letters to between 150 and 300 words. However, many local newspapers publish longer letters if they are well written, or they simply don't have anything better to publish and they need to fill space.

If large newspaper editors like your "hooks," they will edit your letter to fit the available space. I wrote one lengthy letter that was published by using only the first and last paragraphs because they contained good "hooks."

Major papers like the New York Times and the Washington Post edit nearly all of their letters for length, style and content. It seems they don't believe many of us are capable of writing a letter to publish, as-is. At least that has been my experience. And that is why it's important to make your points in the first, middle and last paragraphs.

Not all editors reply to letter submissions, but it doesn't really matter. The only contact that means anything is a request for letter confirmation from someone on the editorial staff. That usually means they are going to publish your letter.

Control the rhetoric

Among other things, rhetoric is defined as the art of effective expression and the persuasive use of language. It is also defined as affected or pretentious language such as political rhetoric. When writing letters to the editor, it is suggested that you control your rhetoric. Do not cross the line from the effective expression of your views to pretentious or inflammatory political rhetoric.

Further, when you feel so strongly about something that you come off sounding like a raving zealot, editors will certainly shy away from your letter. As you read my letters you will notice that I often push that fine line between effective expression and political rhetoric. The trick is to keep it toned down enough to keep it from crossing the line.

Make it interesting

Your point of view should be interesting and educational to the editor and readers. If you are challenging something or someone with opposing facts, be certain to do your homework. You shouldn't just say someone is full of it without backing it up. The best letters that I have read contained something I didn't know.

Say what others are thinking

Editors know when someone writes a letter that says what many readers are thinking. Keep that in mind when you write your letter. Those other people will thank you for it.

Give your letter a title

The best way to grab an editor's attention is with a good title. The title should convey the theme of the letter in a few words similar to newspaper headlines. Editors seldom, if ever, use your title but that's what makes them read your letter over other letters because you're speaking their language.

Reference your letter

As indicated above, if you are writing about something that you read in a newspaper or newsmagazine, make reference to the article, editorial, commentary or letter that you are responding to.

You will have a much better chance at getting your letter published if you join or begin a debate on a major local, state or national issue that is widely published.

Edit and revise your letter

Except for my wife, I don't know anyone who can write a good letter without editing and revising it. I've tried and it seldom works. After you have written the first draft, walk away. Then come back later and read it. You'll often find that it doesn't read nearly as well as you thought when you first wrote it. You may even need to leave it until the next day to re-work it.

Read the letter aloud to yourself or have someone else read it to you to hear how it sounds. If it's easy to read and understand it will probably gain more consideration from editors, and it will be more attractive to your intended audience. Above all, make sure the spelling is correct and that you have condensed the letter as much as possible.

Don't use too many "big words."

If you use too many big words readers might think you're talking down to them. That offends many people and others simply won't be able to understand your message.

One or two well-placed $25 words, however, often helps to drive home your point, and it also attracts the attention of editors.

Timely letters

If you are going to comment on an issue in the news, jump on it while it's hot. With word processors and e-mail, it's much easier to get a letter off to the editor. Most newspapers and newsmagazines accept letters by e-mail. And remember include your address and phone number.

FROM THE TRENCHES OF DEMOCRACY

You may or may not agree with the social, political and economic commentary contained in my letters to the editor. But you will probably agree that letters to the editor are one of the few trenches of democracy from where our voices can be heard by large audiences. Your views regarding local, state, national and global issues are what you should write about.

Call-in radio and television shows provide other mediums to voice your opinion, however, most of them are screened and limited to only a few callers. *C-Span* is unequaled in offering nonpartisan and uncensored telephone access to speak your mind to a great many viewers and listeners throughout the nation.

Fortunately, more and more people are practicing democracy wherever they find it. The Internet has opened up even more avenues. E-mail, forums, conferences, message boards, chat rooms and blog sites offer much more access than ever before.

The media have taken to the Internet with on-line versions of newspapers, radio and television news. Most of them offer access for writing letters to the editor by e-mail. But some limit letters to form submissions. Don't try to write a letter on-line. Compose your letter off-line, then copy and paste it for an on-line submission. You should do the same when posting any lengthy submission.

Television news has grown from brief morning programs and 15 minutes of evening news (50 years ago) to 24 hour instant news. News on the "tube" has become highly competitive. Cable and broadcast news networks pump out whatever they think improves their ratings regardless of how newsworthy it is.

Rather than providing responsible journalism, television news has turned into superficial reporting, entertainment and shock media. Journalistic integrity has been replaced by celebrity journalists and a "chattering class" of pundits.

What was once known as the people's "watch-dogs" has turned into the fame business, condescending elitists, biased politics and rating races. Even though most people get their news from television, the public's trust in television news and much of the print media has plummeted.

ABC, CBS, NBC and CNN are the most biased and the worst violators of the public trust. **ABC**, however, took a leap in the right direction with *20/20's* "Give Me a Break" reporter, John Stossel. His specials exposing the troubling fraud of extreme environmentalism in our schools, the disturbing August 4, 2001 report on America's "Hype" society and the August 11, 2001 report on "Washington" demonstrated ABC's trend-bucking lean in the direction of more responsible journalism.

I wrote a letter ABC commending Stossel and the news division for his special reports. But it didn't last. Stossel took a lot of heat from the liberal establishment, and he was eventually cast out. Even so, he stood fast with his contribution of a series of programs for schools and education. Now, John Stossel has a home with his own show on the Fox News Business Channel.

Fortunately, The Fox News Channel came to dominate cable news with powerful, "fair and balanced" news reporting and analysis. As they say, "We report, you decide."

Still, when it comes to criticism, the liberal news media does not take it very well. Indeed, they give it little more than superficial lip service among themselves from time to time. In the end, however, most of the dominant news media usually just ignore it from their lofty, out-of-touch, perches.

But if we persist in writing well-composed letters we can get their attention. If you want to make an impact, write your letters and send your e-mails to the broadcast networks, cable channels, and to their sponsors. Corporate owners of the news business focus on bottom line profits. Social responsibility is the last thing on their minds. Therefore, the only way to get their attention is by audience complaints and pressure on their corporate advertisers.

Elected representatives usually respond to all letters from their constituents. Unfortunately, their responses are usually shallow pats on the head for being a good, concerned citizen along with a political propaganda pitch. But if they are inundated with a flood of letters and phone calls it does makes a difference, simply because they're always worried about being re-elected.

When writing letters to government agency bureaucrats, especially with complaints, you should address your letter to the head of the agency. It is also helpful to send copies of your letter to your elected representatives and indicate that copies were sent. Many of those department heads are appointed by elected officials.

Writing effective letters can also help you in dealing with personal and business problems including, but not limited to, insurance companies, health care providers, utility companies, banks, credit card companies, lawyers, contractors, and any other business or entity with which you are a client, patient or customer.

Just remember one thing. When writing that letter, start at the top with the president, CEO, manager or business owner. It is much easier than trudging through layers of bureaucracy. You might not get a personal response, but you should get an answer from someone not far down from the top. Even if you don't get a response, rest assured that most letters have some effect.

If you're upset about something, write a letter. It's likely that other people are also upset and have written letters that could have a cumulative effect, which should get someone's attention.

Other than conducting selective polls that only capture people's responses to snapshots about issues, the news media, government and corporate America are woefully out of touch with the people. They are simply clueless about what it's really like out here in the trenches of democracy.

What angers and frustrates most people is being ignored. But if you're persistent in writing effective letters your message will get through. It is my hope and objective to assist you in being heard. **That's what democracy is all about...**

Pep talk

America is hurting and that means us. It's time to re-examine ourselves and do something to make a difference. Though we all have much to deal with in our lives, not much changes unless we make it happen. Many of us feel disenfranchised from government and society.

It is my intention to get you excited about participating in democracy. Get involved by reading books, newspapers and magazines. Watch the news from different sources on television, including *C-Span*. Search the Internet for different views and more information. And compare it all in an effort to find the truth, which seems to be so elusive these days.

Then write those letters. Share what you've learned to help other people find the truth. Write what you feel. Write for justice. Write against injustice. Write for change. Write to support something good. Write to defeat something bad. Complain and criticize, but make it constructive. Identify a problem, but try not to leave it hanging without offering a solution…

CITIZEN'S CORNER

Publish more letters

There is nothing more important or telling about a newspaper than how it handles letters to the editor from its readers.

Two of the most important civil liberties that we possess are "freedom of speech" and "freedom of the press" guaranteed by the First Amendment to the Constitution. It is "my opinion" that a free press should embrace citizens' free speech by publishing more letters to the editor which accurately reflect what is really on their readers' minds. Not just reactions to newspaper stories, editorials and commentary, but people's original thoughts, criticisms, ideas and suggestions.

Local newspapers and publications do a pretty good job of reflecting local opinion about matters of local interest, however, even they could do better. Larger newspapers, newsmagazines and publications have a long way to go to satisfy the public's need to communicate opinion to their fellow citizens, especially when the print media are merging into fewer, impersonal news media giants and conglomerates.

Here's a suggestion for the news media: In addition to publishing letters to the editor, newspaper and newsmagazine editors could select boards of contributors from citizen letter writers to establish what could be called a "Citizen's Corner" in their opinion and editorial sections. Rotating board members could field letters of public interest with brief commentary, which could also include letters of debate over people's legitimate concerns. Indeed, such an approach could go a long way in mending the fractured relationship between people's free speech and the free press — the public and the news media.

LIST OF NEWSPAPERS AND NEWSMAGAZINES

Total account of my published letters in Volumes 1, 2, 4, 5 and 6

(Volume 3 is an account of my unpublished letters, more of which are included in Volumes 4, 5 and 6)

Major newspapers

USA TODAY	68 letters
Los Angeles Times	56 letters
Washington Post	4 letters
New York Times	11 letters
Washington Times	61 letters
Washington Examiner	49 letters
Wall Street Journal	5 letters
Boston Globe	2 letters
New York Post	22 letters
O'Reilly Factor	6 emails

National newsmagazines

Time Magazine	7 letters
U.S. NEWS & World Report	5 letters
Newsweek Magazine	1 letter
L. A. Times Magazine	1 letter
NewsMax Magazine	21 letters

Regional newspapers

The San Bernardino Sun	95 letters
Riverside Press-Enterprise	86 letters
San Diego Union-Tribune (and North County Times)	99 letters
San Francisco Examiner	12 letters
San Francisco Chronicle	8 letters
Sacramento Bee	8 letters
Orange County Register	3 letters

Local newspaper

Victor Valley Daily Press - Press Dispatch	233 letters
VV Daily Press Commentary	1
Apple Valley Review	22 commentaries

Total letters 885

LET'S BEGIN...

The following chapter and letters (listed by year) contain 213 of my published letters to the editor.

Whether or not you agree with the observations and opinions contained in my letters, they should be informative. My letters are written snapshots in time addressing most of the major events and issues over the past 3 years, with emphasis on the 2016 Presidential Election, and my state of California. They are simply one person's take on recent social, economic and political history from the point of view of a common citizen with an uncommon passion.

I sincerely hope the letters will be of interest to you and that they will assist you in writing your own letters. Stay with it and you will get published. As you will see, my letters improved year after year. And as you will discover, there's nothing like seeing your letter in print and knowing that your voice has been heard.

CHAPTER 1:
2015 - 2017 LETTERS

2017 Letters

San Diego Union-Tribune
March 27, 2017

Letting Obamacare implode is right course

It is best that President Trump House Republicans did not have the votes to repeal and replace Obamacare. Indeed, the Unaffordable Careless Act has been well on the road to imploding, as it was destined to do, particularly when it was rammed through the Democrat-controlled Congress from behind closed doors. As incompetent House Speaker, Nancy Pelosi said, "We have to pass it so we will know what's in it."

Surely, after the ACA implodes, the Republican must get their act together and pass enough legislation to help the nation's health care industry get back on its feet and help the American people recover. A good start would be to allow insurance companies to sell health insurance across state lines.

Alas, President Obama's painful legacy will continue to implode and explode as time goes on.

VV Daily Press
March 24, 2017

CBO must go for cooking the books

When President Obama and the Democrat Congress rammed through the phony Unaffordable Careless Act laden with Obama's lies, America's health care was turned upside down and inside out at terrible, unnecessary cost and confusion. An insidious legacy to say the least. Of course, it was substantially the result of the Democrats' puppet OBM and passage from behind doors closed to Republicans – then upheld by a weak Supreme Court.

Now, with the election of President Donald Trump and a Republican-controlled Congress, the prosed repeal of ObamaCareless -- to be replaced with the American Health Care Act -- and the opposing bias of the OMB warning leaving 24 million Americans uninsured, something has to go.

Indeed, the Congressional Budget Office should be eliminated and replaced with private professional budget analysist experts who will provide honest reports instead of the deeply imbedded bureaucrats who have been conditioned to give liberals what they want. And that goes for all Washington bureaucrats who must get their acts together, or leave.

VV Daily Press
March 19, 2017

The hounds of Democrats

Since Donald Trump's election and his concentrated efforts to deliver on his promises to the American people, President Obama, Hillary Clinton and their minions in and out of government – supported by billionaire, George Soros – have launched their "Hounds of Democrats" against President Trump, The Republican Congress and all good, patriotic Americans with a vengeance.

Indeed, President (Premier) Obama's early learning in Communism and the long-term Clinton corruption machine have come to fruition in gathering the storm to undermine and destroy President Trump, his administration and the Congress at any cost. Clearly, the enemy within is alive with social, political and economic sabotage and cancers to accomplish their treasonous madness.

Nevertheless, with God's help, President Trump and true Americans will prevail against all enemies, foreign and domestic.

VV Daily Press
March 15, 2017

Death of Whittier officer

The tragic Feb. 20th death of a Whittier police officer, Keith Boyer at the hands of an active felon gang member is another cop-killing blow to our seriously damaged society at the hands of felon-friendly Governor Jerry Brown and the anti-police former president Obama.

Officer Boyer's remarkable March 3rd, 2017 funeral and burial should serve as a glaring reminder of just how seriously diminished our society has become at the hands of a radicalized socialist Democrat Party, that embraces the bad and condemns law and order – which is clearly un-American.

Indeed, Governor Brown, the Democrat California Legislature and their mindless voters responsible for AB 109 and Proposition 47 releasing criminals to prey upon the people of this blatantly misguided state ought to be ashamed – however, the heartless have no shame.

As a retired deputy sheriff -- who began my long career patrolling the unincorporated East Whittier area in the early 1960's – I am outraged by this and the continuing war against the police. Hopefully, President Trump can turn things around.

Lest we forget, true Americans know and appreciate that the police are our first line of defense. Alas, over three thousand of them attended officer Boyer's funeral.

VV Daily Press
March 9, 2017

Oscars blackmailed

This year's Academy Awards made it painfully clear that Hollywood's African-American activist's 2016 campaign accusing Academy members of racism because of the lack of black Academy members and awards paid-off in 2017 -- with a black Academy President, more board members, more black movies, and blacks winning major acting awards and Best Picture for "Moonlight."

Considering the facts that Best Director, Actor and Actress winners were white, and that Hispanic, Asian and other races were and are grossly under-represented in films, it was obvious that the Academy was clearly "blackmailed."

Black talent notwithstanding, it was sad, but true, including the fact that quality films are increasingly rare throughout increasingly narcissistic Hollywood….

VV Daily Press
March 2, 2017

Illegal Aliens vs. America

Mass national demonstrations by illegal aliens, students and radical Democrat liberals against President Trump are making it painfully clear that the flood of illegals crossing the border taking advantage of former president Obama's failure to enforce immigration laws and granting amnesty to many has significantly increased the numbers of illegal aliens.

Indeed, coupled with Democrat controlled sanctuary cities, illegals are "wagging the dog" of our government and making them more aggressive. So much so, that they are determined to undermine President Trump's determination to enforce the laws.

Worse, the number of criminal illegals crossing the border, have increased gangs, drug trafficking, and criminal predator attacks on American citizens.

Clearly, the daily mass demonstrations shouting that President Trump is "Not my President" and using Trump's effigy as a piñata, cutting off its head, and tearing the body apart, yelling, "tear him apart," is a threat against the President and a federal crime.

Surely, the Democrat/illegal alien war against President Trump and America is anarchy tantamount to treason.

Alas, radical Democrats are giving Democracy a bad name....

VV Daily Press
February 23, 2017

Piranha press

The "Piranha" leftist White House Press Corps and the entire leftist press are proving their intentions to devour President Trump and his administration at any cost, even our national and domestic security and our economy.

Indeed, the loss of President Trump's national security advisor, General Michael Flynn is the first victim of the insidious predators, even though he did nothing illegal in talking with the Russian Ambassador about sanctions during the presidential transition.

Worse, asking for and accepting General Flynn's resignation was the result of treasonous government employee leaks of classified information, which is intolerable, and should be severely dealt with by the attorney general's office forthwith.

Alas, the loss of this highly qualified patriot is a national disgrace.

VV Daily Press
February 17, 2017

Democrats vs. Republicans

Leftist liberal Democrats are making it painfully clear that they are waging a war of political terrorism against newly-elected President

Trump, conservative patriots and the Republican Congress, with relentless personal attacks, mass demonstrations, protests and riots throughout the country, especially in California.

Indeed, with our Constitution, freedoms and liberty at stake, this reckless behavior is becoming a crisis bordering on all-out war, tantamount to treason. Clearly, insidious leaders such as George Soros, Unions, the miseducation establishment, the Pravda-style news media, socialists, extremists and Democrat bosses in the House and Senate are driving the effort with the runaway tyranny of big government and political correctness.

Certainly, the reason behind the upheaval is the time bomb President Obama built over 8 years with his war against police and the rise of Black Lives Matte,, the proliferation of ISIS by ignoring their rapid Middle East and world-wide aggression, and the increases of illegal aliens, crime, drugs and refugees.

Coupled with Mr. Obama's and the Democrat Congress' expansion of intrusive government and control of healthcare, finance and the economy, he has assumed the position of leadership of the indoctrinated enemy within, lit the fuse and left office to ruin America.

VV Daily Press
February 12, 2017

Draining the swamp

As promised, President Trump is in the rapid process of draining the Washington swamp of former president Obama's political snakes and alligators beginning with the resignation of the State Department's entire policy team and the forced resignation of the Border Patrol Chief.

Next, President Trump will slash the work force of EPA regulators and intimidators following his approval of the oil pipelines and restoration of clean coal mining and generation of electric power, along with the exploration of coal, oil and natural gas on federal lands.

Indeed, as expected, President Trump will surely do the same with swamps of the Departments of Energy, mis-Education, Treasury-IRS,

Commerce-SEC. and all other agencies that have preyed upon the American people and business in the United States of free America!

VV Daily Press
February 10, 2017

George Soros: Un-American

Billionaire, George Soros' dirty money is used by the nation's foremost un-American to fund liberal-lice activists and protestors in everything from "Occupy Wall Street" to Black lives matter, insidious liberal news agencies, to the latest college, Hollywood and women's protests against President Trump and his bans on refugees and travelers from terrorist-infested countries – particularly from the Middle East.

Of course Soros ant-American Open Society foundation and illicit activities against our government are most dangerous to our country.

VV Daily Press
January 31, 2017

Enemies of America

Barack Obama and Hillary Clinton lost, John Wayne Trump and the American people won.

Indeed, there's a new Sheriff in our Town, supported by Fox News -- and there's no place for your wars against Wall Street, the police, conservatives, Republicans and regular people waged by Democrats, the media mafia, radical feminists, LGBT's, racists, anarchists, rioters, horrible Hollywood -- or your overbearing government of the liberal elite.

Clearly, you are enemies of the State of America and have no place in our land of the free and home of the brave defenders of our domestic and national security. So, check your scurrilous attacks and insidious guns of indoctrination at the bar of real life, or get out of town!

Yes, that means you, liberal Democrats, Gloria Steinem, Madonna, Ashley Judd, "ugly Betty" and your ilk..... Backed by Ted Turner's CNN Nazi Hitlerites, the Washington Post, New York Times, and sadly, America's former national newspaper, USA TODAY – Nay!

USA TODAY
January 27, 2017

President Trump is taking care of business

With just a week on the job, Trump is taking care of America's business by creating and protecting jobs, securing our borders, protecting our people, and going full speed ahead against our enemies, both foreign and domestic, including the scurrilous enemies within.

Indeed, evil Socialist Democrats and the news media are on the losing side against the forces of good, which will surely prevail under the leadership of Trump, a real President of the United States -- not an imposter like former president Barack Obama, who spent eight years tearing down our country.

Clearly, Trump and his administration are leading the fight to restore America by rebuilding our economy, our defenses, our security, our society, our self-respect, and the overall self-governing power of our people to not only be great again, but greater than ever before.

Words of the day, "Get on board or get out of the way." God bless America, President Trump and the American people.

San Bernardino Sun
January 27, 2017

Forest Service neglect

Re: State of Emergency declared for L.A., San Bernardino and Orange Counties (Jan. 23)

Gov. Jerry Brown declared a state of emergency in California because of excessive rainfall and flooding, especially in burn areas. Of course, the state expects federal government assistance in this serious matter.

However, President Trump, you should review why there were so many out-of-control fires in Forest Service areas because of the gross failures of the Forest Service to respond with appropriate fire-fighting forces, which has been an endemic problem with the Forest Services, even with controlled burns going out of control.

President Trump, the loss of life and property is far too serious to ignore the longtime neglect of the Forest Service, exacerbated by state fire service neglect, particularly in California.

The establishment of fleets of rapid-response DC 10 and Super Scooper water-dropping aircraft throughout California and other states would have gone a long way in preventing runaway brush and forest fires.

VV Daily Press
January 23, 2017

New Sheriff in town

Since President Obama was elected, the liberal media has become the media mafia, with Obama as the anti-American godfather.

Fortunately for USA, there's Fox News and a new sheriff in town named Donald Trump -- and his all-American posse.

San Diego Union-Tribune
January 21, 2017

Readers react to Trump's inauguration

New Sheriff in town
Since President Obama was elected eight years ago, the liberal media has become the media mafia, with Obama as the anti-American

godfather. Fortunately for United States, there's Fox News and a new sheriff in town named Donald Trump -- and his all-American posse.

Donald Trump was just sworn-in as the 45th President of the United States. He will be working tirelessly to give America back to the people who will govern themselves as a government of the people, by the people and for the people.

Ruinous rule by former president Obama and the liberal elite is over. President Trump, his administrative posse and the Republican Congress will protect and defend America against all enemies, foreign and domestic.

Indeed, there is a new Sheriff in town, backed by our Constitution. America will be reformed, recover, prosper and be great again for all of us....

Riverside Press Enterprise
January 20, 2017

President Obama's last days of chaos

President Obama and his administration have made it painfully clear that his last days in office will be consumed by attacking President-Elect Donald Trump, and doing as much more damage to America as he can – along with hateful liberal Democrats in Congress -- leaving a legacy of social, political, economic, anger, division and chaos with our domestic and national security.

Indeed, Mr. Obama's legacy will be replete with an explosion of serious crimes committed by blacks and Hispanics, enormous increases of blacks in movies, television series, commercials and the overall entertainment industry with an emphasis on black lives and open borders as the only things that matter – regardless of the deaths and damages inflicted on society.

Worse, the outgoing president will be responsible for the proliferation of ISIS and terrorism in America and throughout the world – the Florida airport ISIS assassinations, Orlando police officer assassination, the Chicago murder rate, and the vicious racial hate crimes against a mentally disabled white male by four black males and females being the latest cases of hate and violence.

And he says he will remain in Washington to keep up what has become his reckless and ruinous work against America -- with his former attorney general, Eric Holder taking up the defense of California's un-American activities – as the painful beat goes on and on – liberal press included…. Thankfully, our new president, Twitter Trump will be in office soon – hopefully, backed by a Republican Congress with guts!

VV Daily Press
January 16, 2017

Obama's last days of chaos

President Obama and his administration have made it painfully clear that his last days in office will be consumed by attacking President-Elect Donald Trump, and doing as much more damage to America as he can – along with hateful liberal Democrats in Congress -- leaving a legacy of social, political, economic, anger, division and chaos with our domestic and national security.

Indeed, Mr. Obama's legacy will be replete with an explosion of serious crimes committed by blacks and Hispanics, enormous increases of blacks in movies, television series, commercials and the overall entertainment industry with an emphasis on black lives and open borders as the only things that matter – regardless of the deaths and damages inflicted on society.

Worse, the outgoing president will be responsible for the proliferation of ISIS and terrorism in America and throughout the world – the Florida airport ISIS assassinations, Orlando police officer assassination, the Chicago murder rate, and the vicious racial hate crimes against a mentally disabled white male by four black males and females being the latest cases of hate and violence.

And he says he will remain in Washington to keep up what has become his reckless and ruinous work against America -- with his former attorney general, Eric Holder taking up the defense of California's un-American activities – as the painful beat goes on and on – liberal press included.

Thankfully, our new president, Twitter Trump will be in office soon – hopefully, backed by a Republican Congress with guts!

VV Daily Press
January 8, 2017

John Kerry: Un-American

Secretary of State John Kerry proved that he is un-American by his stance against Israel in the United Nations move to condemn Israel's settlements wherein President Obama's administration abstained from the vote. Of course, this is nothing new for Kerry or Obama since they are both anti-American.

Indeed, John Kerry demonstrated being anti-American when, as a member of the U.S. military, he came out against the Viet Nam war testifying against America before Congress. Since then, he became a U.S. Senator, married a wealthy business woman and continued undermining America.

Worse, Kerry stands with President Obama's insidious legacy – with a Democrat Congress -- of war against America's military, economy, healthcare, police, domestic security -- and national security -- by proliferating the rise of radical Islamic terrorism against America and the world.

Fortunately, the American people fought back and elected Donald Trump as the next president. Alas, with President Trump and a Republican Congress, we will survive, recover, be strong and prosper again with true freedom, liberty and the pursuit of happiness.

VV Daily Press
January 2, 2017

Obama and Brown's spite

President Obama has commuted 178 felony prisoners' sentences, and California Gov. Jerry Brown has commuted one felon's sentence and pardoned a total of 1,258 felony prisoners in spiteful acts against the public's interests and safety – striking dangerous blows against our domestic security.

Coupled with AB 109 and Proposition 47, Brown has released thousands of felons to prey upon the people of California.

Even worse, President Obama failed to veto a bad U.N. resolution to spite Israel, while Governor Brown continues to bolster sanctuary cities throughout the state, further endangering our national security against terrorism.

Indeed, the only thing Mr. Obama has left to do against America is to empty Guantanamo and pardon Bergdahl, Manning, and Snowden to secure his destructive legacy against America and the world – not mention doubling the national debt -- while none dare call it treason.

2016 Letters

Riverside Press Enterprise
December 30, 2016

Spiteful actions

President Obama has commuted 178 felony prisoners' sentences, and California Gov. Brown has commuted one felon's sentence and pardoned 112 felony prisoners in spiteful acts against the public's interests and safety — striking dangerous blows against our domestic security.

Worse, Gov. Brown has pardoned 1,258 felons since taking office. Coupled with AB109 and Proposition 47, Brown has released thousands of felons to prey upon the people of California.

Even worse, President Obama rejected a U.N. resolution to spite Israel, while Gov. Brown continues to bolster sanctuary cities throughout the state, further endangering our national security against terrorism.

Indeed, the only thing Mr. Obama has left to do is to empty Guantanamo and pardon Bergdahl, Manning and Snowden to secure his destructive legacy against America and the world — not to mention doubling the national debt — while none dare call it treason.

San Bernardino Sun
December 27, 2016

Releasing prisoners not in society's best interests

President Obama has commuted 178 felony prisoners' sentences and Gov. Jerry Brown has commuted one felon's sentence and pardoned 112 felony prisoners in spiteful acts against the public's interests and safety, striking dangerous blows against our domestic security.

Worse, Gov. Brown has pardoned 1,258 felons since taking office. Coupled with AB109 and Proposition 47, Brown has released thousands of felons to prey upon the people of California.

Even worse, President Obama rejected a U.N. resolution to spite Israel, while Gov. Brown continues to bolster sanctuary cities throughout the state, further endangering our national security against terrorism.

Indeed, the only thing Obama has left to do is empty Guantanamo and pardon Bowe Bergdahl, Chelsea Manning and Edward Snowden to secure his destructive legacy against America and the world — not to mention doubling the national debt — while none dare call it treason.

VV Daily Press
December 25, 2016

President Obama's press conference

President Obama's last press conference was obviously rigged with predetermined questions from the White House (Pravda) Press Corps. All Mr. Obama wanted to talk about was his feigned accomplishments, which were done despite his abuse of power and deceit.

And his press complied with questions about Russia hacking the election, helping Syrian refugees and criticizing President-elect Trump in disguise. Too much for one reporter who fainted.

Indeed, there were no questions or answers about national and domestic security to wit: the deadly world plague of ISIS terrorism, or the American plague of crime and drugs, all created and highly intensified by President Obama's gross failures.

America's worst president, indeed.

Riverside Press Enterprise
December 23, 2016

President Obama's damage

President Obama is bent on doing as much damage to America as he can before leaving office. Indeed, his latest edicts, commutations and pardons are designed to inflict as much damage as possible to the oil industry and America's domestic security.

Coupled with eight years of relentless attacks against America's coal, oil and gas energy resources, releasing criminal predators upon the public, and his war against America's police, he has recklessly inflicted untold damage against our society, our economy and our safety.

Worse, Mr. Obama has intentionally allowed open borders and sanctuary cities and marijuana to flourish, subjecting our people to increased gangs, crime, drugs, murder and the infection of our children without remorse.

Even worse, President Obama has inflicted deadly damage on our national security by blatantly allowing the proliferation of ISIS against the Middle East, America and the world by unleashing relentless attacks against Christians and humanity.

Alas, Obama's last act of defiance will likely be to empty Guantanamo and to pardon blatant traitors Bergdahl, Manning and Snowden.

VV Daily Press
December 19, 2016

Bergdahl pardon?

I believe deserter Sgt. Bowe Bergdahl, who asked President Obama for a pardon, will in fact be pardoned by President Obama on his last day in office. Indeed it will be a national security travesty to pardon a traitor, as it was a far worse act of treason to trade five Taliban terrorist leaders for Bergdahl's release. Surely, considering President Obama is responsible for the proliferation of ISIS and terrorism in the world, he will have been the enemy within during his eight years in office.

VV Daily Press
December 13, 2016

(original letter – unedited. The Dec. 4th letter was edited for space)

California vs. America

State's rights is one thing, however California leaving the union is not idle talk. Indeed, the once golden state has been turned into a dictatorial state with a socialist Democrat governor and supermajority legislature rejecting the U.S. Constitution and federal law – which for all intents and purposes means that it has been a separate nation for a long time – increasingly abusing most of our citizens with punishing taxes and regulations, and a relentless invasion of illegal immigrants, exposing us to an increasing epidemic of crime.

As for the remainder of America, Socialist Democrat President/ King Barrack Obama has done nearly the same thing as California has done in just under 8 years to the other 49 states. Indeed, the first black president has gone to the extremes of making African-Americans superior to all other races, dominating everything with about 14 percent of the population – believing all others are inferior racists.

Indeed, our nation has yet to suffer the full consequences of Mr. Obama's insidious superiority complex reign, which would have been even worse with the insidious superiority complex of the first woman president, Hillary Clinton. Thank God, hopefully, President-elect Donald Trump's "Make America great again' complex and a Republican Congress will save us, our national/domestic security and the country.

Alas, there is little or no hope for Californians.

The Washington Times
December 11, 2016

California has dug own grave

State's rights is one thing, however California leaving the union is not mere idle talk. Indeed, the once golden state has been turned into a dictatorial state with a socialist Democrat governor and super-majority legislature rejecting the U.S. Constitution and federal law. This, for all intents and purposes, means that California has been a separate nation for a long time. It has been increasingly abusing most of our citizens with punishing taxes and regulations, aa well as a relentless invasion of crime-producing illegal immigrants.

As for the remainder of America, in just under eight years socialist Democrat President Obama has done to the other 49 states nearly the same thing. The first black president has gone to the extremes of inciting race wars and essentially treating all non-African-Americans as inferior bigots.

Indeed, our nation has yet to suffer the full consequences of Mr. Obama's insidious superiority complex reign, which would have been continued by a President Hillary Clinton. Hopefully, President-elect Donald Trump's "Make America Great Again' mentality and a Republican Congress will save us, our national security and the country.

Alas, there is little or no hope for Californians.

VV Daily Press
December 4, 2016

California vs. America

State's rights is one thing, however California leaving the union is not idle talk. Indeed, the once golden state has been turned into a dictatorial state with a socialist Democrat governor and supermajority legislature rejecting the U.S. Constitution and federal law – which for all intents and purposes means that it has been a separate nation for a long time – increasingly abusing most of our citizens with punishing taxes and regulations, a relentless invasion of illegal immigrants, exposing us to an increasing epidemic of crime.

As for the remainder of America, Socialist Democrat President/King Barrack Obama has done nearly the same thing as California has done in just under 8 years to the other 49 states. Indeed, the first black president has gone to the extremes of making African-Americans superior to all other races, dominating everything with about 14 percent of the population – believing all others are racist.

Indeed, our nation has yet to suffer the full consequences of his insidious reign, which would have been even worse with the first woman president, Hillary Clinton. Thank God, hopefully, President-elect Donald Trump will save us and the country. Alas, there is little or no hope for Californians.

(original letter - revised)

California vs. America

State's rights is one thing, however California leaving the union is not idle talk. Indeed, the once golden state has been turned into a dictatorial state with a socialist Democrat governor and supermajority legislature rejecting the U.S. Constitution and federal law – which for all intents and purposes means that it has been a separate nation for a long time – increasingly abusing most of our citizens with punishing taxes and regulations, and a relentless invasion of illegal immigrants, exposing us to an increasing epidemic of crime.

As for the remainder of America, Socialist Democrat President/King Barrack Obama has done nearly the same thing as California has done in just under 8 years to the other 49 states. Indeed, the first black president has gone to the extremes of making African-Americans superior to all other races, dominating everything with about 14 percent of the population – believing all others are inferior racists.

Indeed, our nation has yet to suffer the full consequences of Mr. Obama's insidious superiority complex reign, which would have been even worse with the insidious superiority complex of the first woman president, Hillary Clinton. Thank God, hopefully, President-elect

Donald Trump's "Make America great again" complex and a Republican Congress will save us, our national/domestic security and the country.

Alas, there is little or no hope for Californians.

San Diego Union-Tribune
December 2, 2016

Trump should put loyal backers in top spots

Donald Trump's top priorities should be to dump hypocritical Romney from Secretary of State consideration, nominate Gen. David H. Petraeus to the position as a national security warrior secretary of state against ISIS, Syria, Russia and Iran, and pick former New York Mayor Rudolph W. Giuliani as the leader of Homeland Security for our domestic security.

And pick Newt Gingrich as his top White House advisor.

VV Daily Press
December 2, 2016

Stein/Clinton insult voters

It is bad enough that Hillary Clinton sent her supporters on a devious mission to intimidate Donald Trump electors into changing their votes to Clinton.

Now Clinton's failed Green Party candidate, Jill Stein has launched a recount campaign to topple Donald Trump's election in the key states of Wisconsin, Michigan and Pennsylvania, which is undoubtedly at Hillary Clinton's direction and will be joined by Clinton's supporters.

Surely, bitter Hillary Clinton refuses to accept the decision of Trumps electors and voters, even though she said that the only reason she relented and conceded the election was at the urging of President Obama.

All the more reasons that Donald Trump is saving America from Obama's ruinous record and an ultra-dangerous election of Clinton. Indeed, January 20th, 2017 can't come soon enough for America to reform, recover and prosper.

San Bernardino Sun
November 29, 2016

What should be Trump's first priority? More readers weigh in: Letters
Nominate Petraeus

Trump's top priorities should be to dump hypocritical Mitt Romney from secretary of state consideration, and nominate Gen. David Petraeus to the position as a national security warrior and secretary of state against ISIS, Syria, Russia and Iran. And pick Rudy Giuliani as head of Homeland Security.

(original letter – November 29, 2016)

(What should be Trump's top priority? Readers respond to our question: Letters)

Re: Trump's top priority question

Trump's top priorities should be to dump hypocritical Romney from Secretary of State consideration, nominate General Petraeus to the position as a national security warrior secretary of state against ISIS, Syria, Russia and Iran – and pick Rudy Giuliani as the leader of Homeland Security for our domestic security.

As a long time Sun reader, I am deeply concerned about the newspaper asking too many readers questions, publishing only L.A. County responses, and ignoring responses from your historical core of readers from our County of San Bernardino and our Inland Empire. Shame on the San Bernardino Sun.

USA TODAY
November 28, 2016

Calls for a vote recount are just plain desperate

It is bad enough that Hillary Clinton sent her supporters on a mission to intimidate President-elect Donald Trump electors into changing their votes for her, now Jill Stein (the Green Party's presidential candidate) has launched a vote recount campaign in Wisconsin, Michigan and Pennsylvania. This was probably a direction from Clinton to topple Trump's election, which will surely be supported by her followers.

It looks like Clinton refuses to accept the decision of Trump's electors and voters, since it's reported that she conceded the election only after receiving a call from President Obama urging her to do so.

This is all the more evidence that President-elect Trump is saving America from Obama's ruinous record and an ultra-dangerous election of Clinton.

Indeed, Jan. 20, 2017, can't come soon enough for America to reform, recover and prosper.

VV Daily Press
November 25, 2016

From Obama to Trump

During the Clinton-caused economic meltdown and presidential election of 2008, the Democrat Party, and the insidious media, Hollywood and Academia cartel seized on the politically correct opportunity to elect Senator Barrack Obama as the first black president of the United States.

Of course, the cartel knew that President Obama would lead into the two-term tyrannies of overwhelming government together with the first term Democrat Congress establishing forced national health care, the wars on coal energy and finance industry, and unconstitutional wars against small business and hardworking Americans.

Worse, the second term was replete with a war against the police, surrendering the war against terrorism in the Middle East causing the rise of ISIS, terrorist attacks here and around the world, and his deadly deal with nuclear Iran.

Fortunately, the arrogant and un-American cartel failed to elect evil Hillary Clinton as the first woman president.

Indeed, real American states and voters rejected the cartel and the deeply corrupted Clintons, elected the Donald Trump, Mike Pence team, and retained the Republican Congress to bring back America from the edge of social, political and economic ruin. Clearly, there is hope to rebuild and to restore our national and domestic security.

And, to increase our efforts to make America great again – the way we once were, before the Democrats turned to the ruinous socialist devil....

Riverside Press Enterprise
November 24, 2016

From Obama to Trump

During the Clinton-caused economic meltdown and presidential election of 2008, the Democrat Party, and the insidious media, Hollywood and academia cartel seized on the politically correct opportunity to elect Sen. Barrack Obama as the first black president..

Of course, the cartel knew that President Obama would lead into a two-term tyranny of overwhelming government together with the first term Democrat Congress establishing forced national health care and the wars on coal, finance industry, small business and hardworking Americans.

Worse, the second term was replete with a war against the police while surrendering the war against terrorism in the Middle East causing the rise of ISIS, terrorist attacks here and around the world and his deadly deal with nuclear Iran.

Fortunately, the arrogant and un-American cartel failed to elect Hillary Clinton as the first woman president.

Indeed, real American states and voters rejected the cartel and the deeply corrupted Clintons, elected the Donald Trump, Mike Pence team, and retained the Republican Congress to bring back America from the edge of social, political and economic ruin.

Clearly, there is hope to rebuild and to restore our national and domestic security.

We can also increase our efforts to make America great again – the way we once were, before the Democrats turned to ruinous socialism

VV Daily Press
November 17, 2016

Hispanic, radical left anarchy

The core of anarchy, demonstrations, riots and violence against president elect, Donald Trump rests with Hispanics, mostly students and illegals.

Obviously, the anarchy has expanded throughout the country. Most disturbing is the organized Hispanic anarchy in Los Angeles, led by Union Del Barrio furthering the aggression of La Raza, which is intent on taking back California, New Mexico, Texas and the West, taken from Mexico by the Mexican American War.

Indeed, other groups carrying large Mexican flags, they express hatred for the (imperialism) of the U.S. government, including the Obama administration, Hillary Clinton, and of course Donald Trump. Del Barrio organized the current demonstrations in Los Angeles, including the violence.

Considering the vast numbers of Hispanic illegals in America, liberal sanctuary cities, and the fragmented enforcement of the border and ICE, this post presidential election has become a real and present danger to America and our people. Decisive action to preserve national and domestic security is vital.

Worse, anti-American George Soros and his wild Democrat billionaire donor bunch are financing the radical left's anarchy, dangerously exacerbated by the liberal media.

Coupled with California's liberal Democrat government turning a blind eye to the release of criminal illegals from prison, refusing to cooperate with U.S. immigration laws, the legalization of marijuana, punishing taxation against tobacco smokers, the enormous cost if miseducation, and war of treacherous teacher unions' war against non-union charter schools, California taxpayers and the people lose.

USA TODAY
November 14, 2016
(edited in half)

Street demonstrations

Street demonstrations by liberal college students and Hispanics broke out against the election of Donald Trump, which is the defining result of an education system replete with insidious indoctrination of ignorance.

Indeed, when students around the country march in the street shouting "F--- Trump," and "Trump is not my president," it is glaring evidence of socialist political anarchy against America.

President Obama will be gone, and our nation will recover, reform, and prosper under Trump and a Republican Congress.

VV Daily Press
November 13
(unedited)

Liberal anarchy

Street and freeway-blocking demonstrations by mostly liberal college students and Hispanics broke out against the election of Donald Trump, which is the defining result of a miseducation system replete with factories of insidious indoctrination and warehouses of ignorance.

Indeed, when UCLA students march in the street shouting "F---Trump," and other demonstration around the country saying, "Trump is not my president," it is glaring evidence of socialist political anarchy against America, tantamount to treason.

Worse, high school students, mostly Hispanic, left schools and stormed the streets shouting the same hostilities, obviously because of Trump's stand against illegals, sanctuary cities and criminals. Surely, both of those high school and college students should be expelled. Free speech simply doesn't apply.

Clearly, the miseducation system, the misentertainment industry, and the liberal media cartel MPAC should heed the example of President Obama in the civil and cooperative transition of the presidency to president-elect Donald Trump, and face it: The wicked witch, Hillary Clinton is politically dead....

President Obama will be gone, and our nation will recover, reform, and prosper under president Trump and a Republican Congress.

Note: The letter below was written on the first day of demonstrations. Obviously, the anarchy has expanded throughout the country. Most disturbing is the organized Hispanic anarchy led by Union Del Barrio furthering the aggression of La Raza, which is intent on seizing back California and the West, taken from Mexico by the early U.S. government. Indeed, they hate the (imperialism) of the U.S. government, including the Obama administration, Hillary Clinton, and of course Donald Trump. Del Barrio organized the current demonstrations in Los Angeles, including the violence.

San Bernardino Sun
November 12, 2016

Under Trump, U.S. will recover, reform, prosper

Street and freeway-blocking demonstrations by mostly liberal college students and Hispanics broke out against the election of Donald Trump, which is the defining result of a miseducation system replete with factories of insidious indoctrination and warehouses of ignorance.

Indeed, when UCLA students march in the street shouting "F---Trump," and other demonstration around the country saying, "Trump is not my president," it is glaring evidence of socialist political anarchy against America, tantamount to treason.

Clearly, the miseducation and the liberal media cartel should heed the example of President Obama in the civil and cooperative transition of the presidency to president-elect Donald Trump, and face it: The wicked witch, Hillary Clinton is politically dead....

President Obama will be gone, and our nation will recover, reform, and prosper under president Trump and a Republican Congress.

(original letter)

Liberal anarchy

Street and freeway-blocking demonstrations by mostly liberal college students and Hispanics broke out against the election of Donald Trump, which is the defining result of a miseducation system replete with factories of insidious indoctrination and warehouses of ignorance.

Indeed, when UCLA students march in the street shouting "F---Trump," and other demonstration around the country saying, "Trump is not my president," it is glaring evidence of socialist political anarchy against America, tantamount to treason.

Worse, high school students, mostly Hispanic, left schools and stormed the streets shouting the same hostilities, obviously because of Trump's stand against illegals, sanctuary cities and criminals. Surely, both of those high school and college students should be expelled. Free speech simply doesn't apply.

Clearly, the miseducation system, the misentertainment industry, and the liberal media cartel MPAC should heed the example of President Obama in the civil and cooperative transition of the presidency to president-elect Donald Trump, and face it: The wicked witch, Hillary Clinton is politically dead....

President Obama will be gone, and our nation will recover, reform, and prosper under president Trump and a Republican Congress.

The Washington Times
November 3, 2016

Election determines whether destruction continues

Since the election of President Obama, our democratic republic has come increasingly under attack by the liberal media and the politically powerful -- so much so, that we are in eminent danger of losing our national security and our democracy to the evils of socialism.

Though the Republican Party has the majority in Congress, it has been gutted and weakened by wrath of the previous Democrat Party majority of Mr. Obama's first term and that contingent's tyrannical legislation. This has left our country mortally wounded. Mr. Obama's second term has been replete with edicts and executive orders, pouring salt in the wounds and seriously dividing the nation.

If corrupt and criminal Hillary and Bill Clinton are elected co-presidents under the fraud of intimidation and political correctness, we are in danger of continuing the downward spiral. With little hope, the only thing standing in the way of overwhelming socialist power is Republican candidate and freedom fighter Donald Trump. God help us if he and we don't win.

Hopefully, five days from now, we can begin the delivery and recovery of our Constitution, democracy and freedom from evil.

VV Daily Press
November 3, 2016

Campaign chaos

Local, state and federal campaign chaos, exacerbated by biased television news and the press, abounds throughout the nation in this presidential election year like no other.

Indeed, Hillary Clinton has lied, cheated and personally profited throughout her political life bound to be the first woman president, supported by President Obama in his legacy to divide and weaken the nation. He is currently supporting Kamala Harris over the more experienced Loretta Sanchez for California U.S. senator in a racial move, and he is placing Syrian refugees throughout the country without notifying local governments.

In a local San Bernardino County, California campaign for county supervisor, scurrilous Victorville City candidate Angela Valles is attempting to unseat a very competent incumbent, Robert Lovingood by being dishonest and hateful. Surely, Valles is more qualified to work for corrupt Hillary Clinton.

Alas, it's time to take America back with a president Donald Trump, a Republican California U.S. senator, keep Supervisor Lovingood, and send the 23 Syrian refugees planted in Victorville by Mr. Obama back where they came from -- and end the chaos.

VV Daily Press
October 21, 2016

Execution of Sgt. Owen

As a retired law enforcement officer, I am outraged by the execution of Los Angeles County Sheriff's Sgt. Owen by a career criminal who should not have been out of prison. Indeed, it is obvious and frightening that President Obama and California Governor Brown are responsible for the executioner's heinous act because of Obama's war against the police and Brown turning violent criminals loose to prey upon Californians and the American people.

Clearly, Sgt. Owen's blood is on their reckless hands, and those are crimes against society and the people.

Worse, the assassination of many police officers throughout the country has been brought on by President Obama's aggressive Black Lives Matter movement and the Attorney General. It doesn't matter to Mr. Obama or Mr. Brown that the police are the first line of defense against terrorists, invaders and criminals in America.

Of course, the reasons for increased crime is because of President Obama's edicts to release violent federal prisoners. Likewise, Governor Brown's AB 109 – and related legislation -- Proposition 47 and the current ballot initiative, Proposition 57, have and will release thousands of felony state prisoners. Indeed, the public and police are being placed at ever increasing risk.

Surely, both President Obama and Governor Brown must be replaced by responsible people of real character and integrity – federal and state guardians and patriots.

VV Daily Press
October 15, 2016

Vice presidential debate

The vice presidential debate between Pence and Kaine clearly demonstrated that Virginia Senator Tim Kaine is little more than a vicious attack dog for a vicious Hillary Clinton.

On the other hand, Indiana Governor Mike Pence clearly demonstrated that he is solid American of character and integrity qualified to be vice president or president if necessary.

Period!

Riverside Press Enterprise
October 7, 2016

The war on police is anarchy

The insidious war on police fomented by President Obama is anarchy. Recklessly attacking our first line of defense is un-American and places America in danger in these perilous times of terrorism. Indeed, the latest attack, a deputy sheriff's sergeant was shot in Lancaster.

As a retired 41-year veteran in law enforcement and the criminal justice system, I am deeply troubled and offended by what has been going on throughout President Obama's two terms in office, which has put my family and fellow Americans in extreme peril.

Clearly, Mr. Obama is not only responsible for increasing violent crimes and murders, he is responsible for Russian aggression, a nuclear Iran and the proliferation of ISIS and terrorism in the world.

Hopefully, Donald Trump will turn things around and allow America to survive and prosper, instead of Hillary Clinton continuing to steer America down the road to ruin.

VV Daily Press
October 5, 2016

Irresponsible liberal media

President Bush attempted to put a stop to the results, but Barney Frank, Chris Dodd and others stood in his way. Certainly, President Obama has exacerbated <u>the insidious problem, which is leading to another, probably worse, housing and financial collapse.</u>

Slamming Donald Trump comes as no surprise from the liberal media, but when they blindly endorse Hillary Clinton with her history of malfeasance, abuse of power and corruption, that hurts America and the people.

Indeed, the Los Angeles Times front page article, "Scope of Trump's lies unmatched," and their lengthy half page, "An easy decision: Hillary for president," editorial endorsement overlooks Clinton's devious and unlawful conflicts of interests record, that's irresponsible free press.

Clearly, all the dominant liberal media follows suit with extreme political bias, and all have ignored the fact that Bill and Hillary Clinton are responsible for the 2008 housing and financial meltdown caused, not by Wall Street, but by Clinton's administration forcing banks and mortgage lenders to give unaffordable home loans to unqualified home buyers.

President Bush attempted to put a stop to the results, but Barney Frank, Chris Dodd and others stood in his way. Certainly, President

Obama has exacerbated the insidious problem, which is leading to another, probably worse, housing and financial collapse.

America must have relief from all this, and the expansion of world terrorism caused by Obama and Hillary Clinton. Donald Trump and a strong Republican Congress is our only hope.

San Diego Union-Tribune
October 1, 2016

Presidential debate reaction

In the first Hillary Clinton – Donald Trump debate, each candidate displayed the roots of their character. Donald Trump was brash and to the point, and Hillary Clinton was condescending and arrogant.

The main different between them is that Trump is a very successful businessman, and Hillary Clinton is a slick politician with a history of political corruption, abuse of power and extreme greed.

In terms of their goals, Trump wants to save America and make it great again. Clinton expects a coronation as the first woman president and to rule as queen of America down the road to ruin.

What was missing from the debate, was the fact that Clinton and Obama are responsible for the proliferation of ISIS, and Russian aggression, and that Bill Clinton is responsible for the 2008 housing and financial collapse.

Riverside Press Enterprise
September 30, 2016

Round one went as expected

In the first Hillary Clinton – Donald Trump debate, each candidate displayed the roots of their character. Donald Trump was brash and to the point, and Hillary Clinton was condescending and arrogant.

The main different between them is that Trump is a very success-ful businessman, and Hillary Clinton is a slick politician with a history of political corruption, abuse of power and extreme greed.

In terms of their goals, Trump wants to save America and make it great again. Clinton expects a coronation as the first woman presi-dent and to rule as queen of America down the road to ruin.

What was missing from the debate, was the fact that Clinton and Obama are responsible for the proliferation of ISIS, nuclear weapons and Russian aggression, and that Bill Clinton is responsible for the 2008 housing and financial collapse.

VV Daily Press
September 29, 2016
Your View: Readers weigh in on first Trump-Clinton debate

Clinton - Trump debate

In the first Hillary Clinton – Donald Trump debate, each candidate displayed the roots of their character. Donald Trump was brash and to the point, and Hillary Clinton was condescending and arrogant.

The main different between them is that Trump is a very success-ful businessman, and Hillary Clinton is a slick politician with a history of political corruption, abuse of power and extreme greed.

In terms of their goals, Trump wants to save America and make it great again. Clinton expects a coronation as the first woman presi-dent and to rule as queen of America down the road to ruin.

What was missing from the debate, was the fact that Clinton and Obama are responsible for the proliferation of ISIS, nuclear weapons and Russian aggression, and that Bill Clinton is responsible for the 2008 housing and financial collapse.

The Washington Times
September 27, 2016

Trump must save us from Clinton

Slamming Donald Trump is nothing new for the liberal media, but when it blindly endorse Hillary Clinton. who has a history of malfeasance, abuse of power and corruption, they hurt America and the people.

Indeed, the Los Angeles Times front page article, "Scope of Trump's lies unmatched," and their lengthy half page, "An easy decision: Hillary for president," editorial endorsement overlooks Clinton's devious and unlawful conflicts of interests, that's irresponsible free press.

Clearly, all the dominant liberal media follows suit with extreme political bias, and all have ignored the fact that Bill and Hillary Clinton are responsible for the 2008 housing and financial meltdown. That's right -- it was caused, not by Wall Street, but by Clinton's administration forcing banks and mortgage lenders to give unaffordable home loans to unqualified home buyers.

President George W. Bush attempted to put a stop to the results, but congressmen Barney Frank, Chris Dodd and others stood in his way. Certainly, President Obama has exacerbated the insidious problem, which is leading to another, probably worse, housing and financial collapse.

America must have relief from all this and the expansion of world terrorism caused by Mr. Obama and Mrs. Hillary Clinton. Donald Trump and a strong Republican Congress are our only hope.

VV Daily Press
September 27, 2016

O.J. Injustice dominates Emmys

The insidious injustice of O.J Simpson getting away with a vicious double murder honored by dominating the Emmy Awards comes as no surprise, as it headlines the reckless decline of the entertainment industry.

Indeed, Hollywood has become a superficial society of social aggression, political tyranny, selfish interests and extremes of shallow minds, absent social redeeming value.

Coupled with damaging violence, lazy remakes, true stories without core truth, stupid sit-coms and soaps, overdone cop, legal and medical series, and the obsession with horror, apocalypse and superhero movies, Hollywood has turned into a tasteless entertainment wasteland.

Add the irresponsibility of television commercials depicting loud, obnoxious behavior, idiotic situations and reckless speeding cars to the equation, and there isn't much left but mind-numbing experiences....

The Washington Times
September 21, 2016

Emmys show Hollywood's decline

The insidious injustice of O.J. Simpson getting away with a vicious double murder honored by dominating the Emmy Awards comes as no surprise, as it headlines the reckless decline of the entertainment industry.

Indeed, Hollywood has become a superficial society of social aggression, political tyranny, selfish interests and extremes of shallow minds, absent social redeeming value.

Coupled with damaging violence, lazy remakes, true stories without core truth, stupid situation comedies and soaps, overdone cop, legal and medical series, and the obsession with horror, apocalypse and superhero movies, Hollywood has turned into a tasteless entertainment wasteland.

Add the irresponsibility of television commercials depicting loud, obnoxious behavior, idiotic situations and reckless speeding cars to the equation and there isn't much left but mind-numbing experiences.

San Diego Union-Tribune
September 20, 2016

O.J. Emmys highlight decline of television

The insidious injustice of O.J. Simpson getting away with a vicious double murder honored by dominating the Emmy Awards comes as no surprise, as it headlines the reckless decline of the entertainment industry.

Indeed, Hollywood has become a superficial society of social aggression, political tyranny, selfish interests and extremes of shallow minds, absent social redeeming value.

Coupled with damaging violence, lazy remakes, true stories without core truth, stupid situation comedies and soaps, overdone cop, legal and medical series, and the obsession with horror, apocalypse and superhero movies, Hollywood has turned into a tasteless entertainment wasteland.

Add the irresponsibility of television commercials depicting loud, obnoxious behavior, idiotic situations and reckless speeding cars to the equation and there isn't much left but mind-numbing experiences.

VV Daily Press
September 15, 2016

Climate and criminal cartel

It's bad enough that President Obama has exacted serious climate change hoax damage against our energy resources and our economy with his war against coal and oil energy, with irresponsible measures and far-reaching consequences.

However, Governor Brown and the Democrat California Legislature cartel refuse to be outdone the president, when they take climate change legislation to astronomic extremes that will seriously damage our California's economy and our people.

Indeed, Brown is extending AB 32 Cap and Trade into the stratosphere with SB32 and AB197 wherein it will put California crashing into high gear. Surely, reckless climate change legislation is signing a death warrant that will raise the cost of living and send the state into economic oblivion.

Coupled with Brown releasing criminals to prey upon the people, it's a Brown climate and criminal cartel. The people are the victims and they lose....

Riverside Press Enterprise
September 13, 2016

State should butt out of cigarette taxes

It was bad enough that Rob Reiner's punishing 50 cents per pack tobacco tax proposition passed, and has been used for everything but tobacco-related health problems.

Now, smokers are expected to believe that Proposition 56's tyrannical $2.00 per pack tax will be used for public health, when in fact it will be just another cash cow for the state. Inflicted upon those who can least afford the tax.

Worse, the legalization of marijuana proposition will surely be passed and become another cash cow for the state, even though it is a gateway to hard drugs. Indeed, it doesn't matter that the black market for cigarettes and crime will escalate because of both propositions.

Alas, traveling down the liberal road to punishing use of a legal product, while recklessly approving use of an illegal drug for taxes is unconscionable and amounts to little more than voter-assisted social, political and economic suicide....

VV Daily Press
September 4, 2016

Wrecking crew against America

President Obama, Hillary and Bill Clinton, and Governor Brown are the primary wrecking crew against America, as follows:

President Obama has damaged the freedoms of Americans with the reckless, unconstitutional actions against our economy, our energy resources, our national security and our domestic security with executive orders and edicts, wars against coal and oil, finance, healthcare, the police – diminishing our border security, military defenses, allowing the proliferation of ISIS terrorism – releasing criminals to prey on the people, and imposing punishing regulations and taxes.

As Secretary of State, Hillary Clinton participated in the proliferation of ISIS terrorism, and used and abused her office for the Clinton Foundation and personal gain. As a candidate for president, she intends to assign the economy to her former president husband, Bill Clinton, who is directly responsible for the 2008 economic collapse, by forcing banks and mortgage lenders to give unaffordable home loans to unqualified buyers in mass.

California Governor Jerry Brown is a major player in the wrecking crew against California and America with economy-busting, punishing taxation, regulations, bullet train and water tunnel bond scams, $billions in the miseducation of students, high energy costs, releasing criminals to prey on Californians, lack of border security, support of sanctuary cities, and threats to our national and domestic security.

Indeed, the unconscionable Democrat Party and the liberal press covers for the un-American trio and all who support continued attacks against the people. Attention voters: wise up and don't commit voter-assisted suicide by electing or re-electing more of the same poison to our freedom and liberty.

Alas, that they're doing is tantamount to treason....

VV Daily Press
August 28, 2016

The economic collapse bomb

Before it's too late, Donald Trump should drop the 2008 economic collapse bomb on Bill Clinton for causing it.

Indeed, Clinton caused the meltdown by using HUD's Andrew Cuomo and AG Janet Reno to intimidate banks and mortgage lenders to provide unaffordable home loans to unqualified buyers, mainly African Americans, who defaulted on their loans in mass.

Wall Street did not cause the collapse, they simply attempted to survive Fannie Mae's and Freddie Macs compliance with Clinton's mandate by bundling good and bad loans.

Bill Clinton was the risk-taking presidential bad guy in the 2008 crash, not George W. Bush. He tried to stop it, but Barney Frank and Chris Dodd stood in his way. Worse, If elected, Hillary Clinton intends to put Bill in charge of the economy.

The insidious liberal media has ignored the truth and has been protecting him all this time. And the conservative media has dropped the ball. It's past time for voters to know it, and hold Clinton and the media responsible for the damage to the economy and America.

But wait, it's not over. Eight years of President Obama has America on crash course for and even worse economic train wreck....

VV Daily Press
August 18, 2016

Super Scoopers are a magic bullet

Though my California Burning letters focused on the DC-10 first response firefighting capabilities, I realize that they cannot be used in all first responses. And I meant no disrespect to firefighters.

Indeed, my 41 year career in law enforcement and the criminal justice system included 3 years as the lead fire dispatcher with the RFPA Desert Com, in which I had firsthand experience with wildfires in the High Desert and local mountain areas.

I also had experience as a deputy sheriff in an L.A County Sheriff's fire road camp providing security for inmate fire crews on the front lines of several fires. I sincerely apologize to anyone who was offended.

My concerns are directed at U.S. Forest Service mismanagement of wildfires, and to a point with Cal Fire. The current crisis is the Pilot Fire, which could have been extinguished by Super Scoopers with Silverwood Lake water sources, while it was growing from 20 acres, before it went out of control to over 7000 acres.

Worse, the smoke from massive wildfires adversely affects thousands, hundreds of thousands, even millions of people. Particularly, those with respiratory problems – my wife and I among them – who are generally exposed or confined to our homes with air conditioning to survive under those conditions.

The point is, there is no reason why the Forest Service and Cal Fire could not have previously purchased or built Super Scoopers like Canada did, to be widely distributed for immediate response -- in the Pilot Fire case -- dispatched from the Victorville Logistics Base, and or Norton.

Surely, Super Scoopers would be the magic bullet. Certainly, the Forest Service failed to call in a heavy response to the Station Fire, and Governor Brown could have provided funding for Super Scoopers instead of his wasteful bullet train and other state boondoggles....

Again, I appreciate all firefighters. I have family in the fire service, and family who resides in the threatened area of Arrowhead Lake Road, so my concerns are also personal.

VV Daily Press
August 14, 2016

Liberal media cartel vs. Donald Trump

The worst enemies to America's constitutionals freedoms are President Obama, Hillary Clinton, congressional Democrats and the liberal media cartel that supports them. Indeed, under the Obama administration, our social, political, economic, domestic and national security are at all-time lows.

Clearly, the liberal media has abdicated their freedom of the press responsibilities for fair and objective reporting. Instead they have chosen a path similar to Russia's state media, Pravda under the direction of overbearing government that violates the people's freedoms, and attacks any resistance.

Surely, the only way America's future can be protected against intrusive, domineering government, and a world wrought with terrorism will be to reject a continued Obama regime with Hillary Clinton, elect Republican Donald Trump president and increase Republican majorities in the House and Senate.

And the only way that will happen is if voters wise-up to the media cartel's relentless attacks against Donald Trump and reject Hillary Clinton's history of corruption. Otherwise, the 2016 presidential election will result in voter-assisted suicide.

San Diego Union-Tribune
August 6, 2016

Obama should not be promoting Clinton

The only reason President Obama is supporting Hillary Clinton is to secure his social, political and economic legacy, which has been corrosive and destructive to America with enormous economic and national security consequences, just as Hillary Clinton's will be if she is elected president. To elect her would be voter-assisted- suicide....

Donald Trump should ignore insidious attacks on him as baiting, which is exactly what Hillary Clinton is doing. Trump should simply stick to his message and clarify what he intends to do as president.

Indeed, President Obama is completely out of line taking his support of Hillary Clinton to attacking Donald Trump, which outgoing presidents just don't do. They finish their term(s) and quietly leave.

Unfortunately, Obama intends to do otherwise for his personal ambitions beyond his presidency. Taxpayers should not be required to pay for that....

Riverside Press Enterprise
August 5, 2016

President Obama is out of line

The only reason President Obama is supporting Hillary Clinton is to secure his social, political and economic legacy, which has been corrosive and destructive to America -- just as Hillary Clinton's legacy will be if she is elected president. To elect her would be voter-assisted suicide.

Donald Trump should ignore insidious attacks on him as baiting, which is exactly what Hillary Clinton is doing. Trump should simply stick to his message and clarify what he intends to do as president.

Indeed, President Obama is completely out of line taking his support of Hillary Clinton to attacking Trump, which outgoing president just don't do. They finish their term(s) and quietly leave..

Unfortunately, Obama intends to do otherwise for his personal ambitions beyond his presidency.

California burning

Immediate use of DC-10 water drops would have extinguished the Sand Fire brush fire along the 14 freeway before it spread into an out-of-control wildfire.

Indeed, with the history of firefighting incompetence by the U.S. Forest Service and Cal Fire at Lake Arrowhead, the Cajon Pass into the Victor Valley, Santa Barbara, San Gabriel Canyon, Lake Isabella, and many fires in Northern California, needless loss of forest lands, property and lives could have been simply prevented.

Clearly, all of these wildfires and more across the county could have been prevented by a fleet of DC-10 tankers subject to immediate dispatch with enormous water drops at the start of each fire, extinguishing them before they spread.

Surely, waiting until fire get out of control, then sending DC-10's to drop red Fosh-Chek slurry to keep out of control fires from spreading further is nothing more than an exercise in futility. Particularly, after thousands of firefighters, equipment and millions of taxpayer dollars are wasted.

Alas, it's beyond time to get it right with a vastly distributed fleet of DC-10's loaded with water and waiting for the call to keep California and America from burning.

VV Daily Press
July 24, 2016

Obama insults Dallas police

President Obama's carefully articulated sermon at the memorial for the 5 assassinated Dallas police officers was nothing more than a veiled attempt to justify his underlying contempt for law enforcement -- our first line of defense -- the rule of law and America.

Considering President Obama's divisive history with race relations, and his hateful war against the police, at this point, it's gone too far. Indeed, he must pull back the militant Black Lives Matter movement for the good of the nation before it's too late.

Surely, it's painfully clear that President Obama is losing the war against terrorism, and winning the war against the police, which is tantamount to treason.

Riverside Press Enterprise
July 21, 2016

Trump made right choice with Pence

Donald Trump made a good choice of Mike Pence as his VP running mate. When he wins the election, he should choose Newt Gingrich as his chief of staff, Chris Christie as Attorney General, Rudy Giuliani as director of Homeland Security, Lt, Gen. Michael Flynn as Secretary of Defense, and Ben Carson as Surgeon General director of HHS for a good start.

However, it should be noted that Hillary Clinton calling Mike Pence the most extremist VP choice in a generation, and the Democrat national media nitpicking Trump's wife for plagiarizing Obama's wife's comments at their nominating conventions, is as politically stupid and low as you can get.

Indeed, there is no comparison between true American conservative Pence and Hillary's potential VP un-American choice of Communist Elizabeth Warren. And surely, valuing your parents moral advice is meaningful. The difference is, Trump's wife meant it. Obama's wife did not.

Riverside Press Enterprise
July 12, 2016

President Obama's sermon insults Dallas police

President Obama's carefully articulated sermon at the memorial for the five assassinated Dallas police officers was nothing more than a veiled attempt to justify his underlying contempt for law enforcement – the rule of law's first line of defense.

Considering President Obama's divisive history with race relations, and his hateful war against the police, at this point, it's gone too far. Indeed, he must pull back the militant Black Lives Matter movement for the good of the nation before it's too late.

Surely, it's painfully clear that President Obama is losing the war against terrorism, and winning the war against the police, which is tantamount to treason.

VV Daily Press
July 3, 2016

Kamala Harris should resign

California Attorney General Kamala Harris is a contemptible political opportunist. Her recent announcement to investigate the contemptible incompetence of San Bernardino County's Children and Family Services, responsible for the child abuse, torturing and killing of children, is too little and very late in coming.

Indeed, the only reason Harris is taking action now, is to further her campaign to replace Barbara Boxer as U.S. Senator for California. Question is, where was the Attorney General over a year ago when a

Channel 11 Fox News completed an investigation into the insidious situation over a year ago?

Surely, Harris' misfeasance that contributed to the pain, suffering and death of innocent children is more than sufficient evidence that she is not fit to be Attorney General -- certainly not a U.S. Senator -- and that she should resign from office immediately.

Riverside Press Enterprise
June 30, 2016

How to stop California from burning

What does it take to get letter published with the answer to fighting California wildfires?

Indeed, with the history of firefighting incompetence by the U.S. Forest Service and Cal Fire at Lake Arrowhead, the Cajon Pass into the Victor Valley, Santa Barbara, San Gabriel Canyon, Lake Isabella, and many fires in Northern California, needless loss of forest lands, property and lives could have been simply prevented.

Clearly, all of these wildfires and more across the county could have been prevented by a fleet of DC-10 tankers subject to immediate dispatch with enormous water drops at the start of each fire, extinguishing them before they spread.

Surely, waiting until fire get out of control, then sending DC-10's to keep out of control fires from spreading further is nothing more than an exercise in futility. Particularly, after thousands of firefighters, equipment and millions of taxpayer dollars are wasted.

It's beyond time to get it right to keep California from burning.

Riverside Press Enterprise
June 27, 2016

AG Harris is doing too little, too late

California Attorney General Kamala Harris is a political opportunist.

Her recent announcement to investigate the incompetence of San Bernardino County's Children and Family Services, responsible for the child abuse, torturing and killing of children, is too little and very late in coming.

Indeed, the only reason Harris is taking action now, is to further her campaign to replace Barbara Boxer as U.S. Senator for California.

Question is, where was the Attorney General over a year ago when a Channel 11 Fox News completed an investigation into the insidious situation over a year ago?

Surely, Harris' misfeasance that contributed to the pain, suffering and death of innocent children is more than sufficient evidence that she is not fit to be Attorney General -- certainly not a U.S. Senator -- and that she should resign from office immediately.

VV Daily Press
June 23, 2016

One America News Network

Overwhelmed by major event news feeding frenzies and saturation coverage on all Local and national television news networks, such as the Orlando tragedy and presidential election at the expense of other news?

There is relief from all that contained on this no nonsense cable news network: The One America News Network with productions from California and Washington D.C. Indeed, One America News is professional journalism that covers local, state, national and international news without dwelling on it like the superficial chattering class of the biased national news media, with the exception of Fox News.

One America News is free from relentless commercials, comprehensive, informative, educational (replete with American history) and refreshingly to the point with its coverage. I highly recommend it to everyone.

VV Daily Press
June 16, 2016

Hillary Clinton, absolute power

Hillary Clinton's insidious career is replete with an obsessive drive for absolute power, from her conflicts of interest power grabs as first lady, to the Clinton Foundation, to running for president against Barrack Obama, to Obama's Secretary of State, and her ultimate grab for absolute power as the first woman president of the United States.

Problem is, as Barrack Obama was the worst choice for the first black president of America – deeply damaging our country -- Hillary Clinton would be the worst choice for the first woman president – potentially damaging our country beyond repair and recovery.

Indeed, as it has always been known tyrants are developed on the premise that absolute power corrupts absolutely, Obama has proved the premise and now Clinton promises to join those absolutely destructive ranks.

Worse, President Obama has openly diminished our economy, domestic security and national security. Likewise, Hillary Clinton has unjustly enriched herself using her position of secretary of state, and she has criminally violated our national security with her personal emails.

Surely, the American people cannot be seduced into electing such a corrupt parasite. Particularly, when she intends to put her husband, Bill Clinton in charge of the economy. You know, the president Clinton who caused the economy to crash in 2008!

The Washington Times
June 13, 2016

To save U.S., back Trump

Mitt Romney's scathing remarks against Donald Trump's competency to be president are hypocritical to say the least – particularly given that in 2012 Romney betrayed the Republican Party in his feckless presidential debate against President Obama.

Indeed, even though Obama lied about calling Benghazi a terror attack, his assertion that he did call it an act of terror was supported by highly partisan CNN debate moderator Candy Crowley -- without serious objection from Mr. Romney. This was a cowardly act proving he was no match for Mr. Obama. Clearly, Mr. Romney was not up to defeating Mr. Obama or stopping Mr. Obama's corrosive path against our national security and economy.

Surely, Donald Trump is a political phenomenon in this 2016 election against Hillary Clinton, but he has what it takes to win and recover our economy and domestic security. However, and America's chances will be seriously reduced if disorganized Republican leaders don't get their act together, defeat Clinton and increase Republican control of Congress.

Alas, if they don't it will be a cowardly betrayal of America and our people. I wasted my vote for Mr. Romney in 2012. My vote for Mr. Trump will not be wasted.

Daniel B. Jeffs
Apple Valley, Calif.

(Original letter)

Mitt Romney's Republican Party betrayal

Mitt Romney's scathing remarks against Donald Trump's competency to be president are hypocritical to say the least, particularly when Mr. Romney betrayed the Republican Party in his feckless 2012 presidential debate against President Obama regarding the Benghazi terrorist attack.

Indeed, even though Obama lied about calling Benghazi a terror attack, supported by his administration, including secretary of state, Hillary Clinton, his assertion that he did call it an act of terror, was supported by highly partisan CNN debate moderator, Candy Crowley, without serious objection from Romney.

Clearly, it was a cowardly act proving he was no match for President Obama, which throughout the campaign was a betrayal of the Republican Party and the American people. Certainly, Romney was not up to defeating Obama and stopping Obama's corrosive path against our national security, our domestic security and our economy.

Surely, Donald Trump is a political phenomenon in this 2016 election against Hillary Clinton, but he has what it takes to win and recover our economy, national security and domestic security. However, his chances and America's chances will be seriously reduced if seriously disorganized Republican leaders don't get their act together, defeat Clinton and increase Republican control of Congress.

VV Daily Press
June 9, 2016

Rising threats, shrinking military

Bret Bair's Fox News Special Report regarding America's Rising Threat, Shrinking Military is a comprehensive dire warning about President Obama's perilous national security legacy of causing the rise of violence and terrorism in the world, dangerously shrinking our military, and the rising of threats to America from, Russia, China and North Korea.

Indeed, because of President Obama's long record of divisions -- attacking our society, our economy and our freedoms -- and his overall contempt for America, supported by the liberal media and Democrat Party, he has recklessly placed our country and our people in extreme debt and danger.

Therefore, at the end of his destructive terms in office, he must be replaced by a strong, qualified Republican patriot in the November presidential election. At this time, the nominee to restore America is Donald Trump.

VV Daily Press
June 2, 2016

California socialists vs. America

Presidential candidates Hillary Clinton, Bernie Sanders, indoctrinated students, unions, illegal aliens and the Socialist State of California have made is painfully and violently clear that Republican candidate, Donald Trump, is an enemy of the socialist state.

Indeed, America is already in deep trouble because of President Obama's 7 ½-year socialist assault on our Constitution, our free society, our free market economy, our domestic security and our national security.

So, it's now a matter of a political war between anti-American socialists and Republican freedom fighters, currently being led Donald Trump for our survival as true constitutional democratic republic.

Attention voters: Vote for freedom and recovery. Not for giving up to socialism and surrendering to terrorism. Don't be a fool!

The Washington Times
May 30, 2016

Culture warriors can save U.S.

As President Obama's corrosive legacy continues to bulldoze the best interests of the American people, we are painfully reminded of just how insidious overwhelming government can be. It is not so different from the tyrannical government that inspired the American Revolution.

Indeed, Mr. Obama's arrogant monarchial reign and reckless, narcissistic pursuit of a legacy has been bent on increasing government attacks on our social, political and economic freedoms with unconstitutional executive orders, taxes and regulations. Worse, Mr. Obama has been undermining our economic security with his "climate change" hoax and its wars on oil, coal and natural gas in favor of costly and unreliable solar and wind. This constitutes an overall attack on our economy and cost of living.

Even worse, President Obama has divided our nation, conducted a wars on the police and our domestic security, and critically compromised our national defense, military strength and readiness. His expanding romance with Communist nations – Russia, China, Cuba and Viet Nam -- is surpassed only by his record of allowing the unbridled growth of the Taliban, al-Qaeda, ISIS, and the Muslim Brotherhood.

Our only hope after President Obama's 8-year war on America, is to reject the continued socialism of Clinton/Sanders and elect conservatives to government. Otherwise we will be committing voter-assisted social, political and economic suicide.

Unfortunately, most of my state of California has long been in the forefront of socialism, with overbearing government attacking the people and business with punishing taxes and regulations, and allowing crime to flourish. Fortunately, there is an island of hope in most of San Bernardino and our Victor Valley high desert community. Here have solid conservatives both in office and running for office, which is comforting in a world fraught with fear and evil.

Hopefully, there are enough culture warriors remaining our country to overcome our enemies. This November, vote Trump and vote Republican.

San Bernardino Sun
May 25, 2016

Donald Trump's economic plans will help U.S.

This will surely be a vicious presidential election. Still, the liberal press is intentionally being irresponsible to voters by not truthfully covering Hillary Clinton's statements about her husband taking over a large part of the presidential portfolio, including being the economy czar. Particularly, with Bill Clinton's destructive record of causing the 2008 economic meltdown.

It's simply a matter of choosing either socialism or democracy, leaving successful businessman, Donald Trump as the only choice to save America's economy, domestic and national security, and our freedom. Indeed, freedom from Clinton's and Obama's corrosive legacies.

VV Daily Press
May 25, 2016

(Unedited)

Clinton's economic record

In a recent campaign speech Hillary Clinton indicated that if elected president, her husband, Bill would assume large part of the presidential portfolio. She said that she would put him in charge of stimulating the economy because, "you know he knows how to do that." Problem is, he knows how to do just the opposite.

Indeed, when Bill Clinton ran for president in 1992, he campaigned against George HW Bush's economic recession, with the mantra, "It's the economy, stupid." When in reality, the economy was coming out of a natural recovery from a recession. So, it was a stupid political lie to get votes, of course.

Personal attacks aside, what really matters about the Clintons is what former president Bill Clinton did in his second term to cause the collapse of housing and finance by forcing banks and mortgage lenders to give home loans to unqualified buyers -- based upon his devious drive to do overcome "redlining" against black home buyers -- which expanded to national, unchecked mass of unqualified buyers and the real cause of the economic meltdown.

Clearly, Bill Clinton and his hit squad of AG, Janet Reno, HUD Director, Andrew Cuomo, and Fannie Mae chairman, Franklin Raines are totally responsible for the 2008 housing and finance bust, not President George W. Bush or Wall Street. Indeed, an economic bust which President Obama has exacerbated throughout his terms in office.

Alas, no one is talking about the real cause of the housing and financial crisis, especially the irresponsible, biased press. Clearly, if Hillary Clinton is elected, it would not only be economic suicide, it would be a Benghazi-style national security disaster.

Riverside Press Enterprise
May 20, 2016

Clinton and the meltdown

In a recent campaign speech, Hillary Clinton indicated that if she is elected president, she would put her husband, Bill, in charge of stimulating the economy because, "you know he knows how to do that." Problem is, he knows how to do just the opposite.

Indeed, when Bill Clinton ran for president in 1992, he campaigned against George H.W. Bush's economic recession, with the mantra, "It's the economy, stupid." When in reality, the economy was coming out of a natural recovery from a recession.

What really matters about the Clintons is what Bill Clinton did in his second term by forcing banks and mortgage lenders to give home loans to unqualified buyers -- based upon his devious drive to do overcome "redlining" against black homebuyers -- which produced a mass of unqualified buyers and the real cause of the economic meltdown.

Clearly, Bill Clinton and his hit squad of Attorney General Janet Reno, HUD Secretary Andrew Cuomo and Fannie Mae Chairman, Franklin Raines are totally responsible for the 2008 housing and finance bust, not President George W. Bush or Wall Street.

Clearly, if Hillary Clinton is elected, it would not only be economic suicide, it would be a Benghazi-style national security disaster.

VV Daily Press
May 15, 2016

President Trump

Republican presidential candidate Donald Trump is an accomplished, tough patriot and can win the election if he does it right.

Indeed, by picking the right running mate and Cabinet, Donald Trump could easily become our next President:

Vice President, John Kasich

Secretary of State, Mike Huckabee

Secretary of Defense, should be the most competent general in our military

Attorney General, Chris Christie

Secretary of Homeland Security, Rudy Giuliani

Secretary of Health and Human Services, Dr. Ben Carson

Secretary of Education, Scott Walker

Secretary of the Treasury, Carly Fiorina

Etc.

Above all, Trump and his prospective administration must prevent Hillary Clinton from finishing President Obama's take down of America. And in doing so, Trump must generate big coat tails to increase Republican majorities in the House and Senate.

Surely, it's past time for a recovery from selfish-interest liberal disintegration, and an Obama-led domestic and national security disaster. Indeed, we must have a Trump-led conservative restoration of America, before it's too late....

Note: I have since changed the VP pick to Newt Gingrich.

VV Daily Press
May 2, 2106

Canceling papers, keeping Daily Press

For years, I have subscribed to print newspapers with a focus on major news stories and what is going on in my community, region, state, country and the world. And my main focus has been the opinion pages. I also subscribe to the Washington Post and New York Times online, along with the Orange County Register and Riverside Press Enterprise.

I realize that newspapers have been struggling because of online news via the Internet. Television news notwithstanding, I have kept informed with great interest. Unfortunately, the news has become so biased, that the American people have been dangerously misinformed.

Indeed, if it were not for Fox News and the few honest, conservative traditional newspapers, Americans would be fully indoctrinated against themselves and seriously against their interests of liberty, freedom and self-determination.

Getting to the point of this letter, I now feel betrayed by my newspapers, particularly, the L.A. Times, USA TODAY, the San Bernardino Sun, the Washington Post and New York Times online, and sadly, the Wall Street Journal.

Therefore, I cancelled my L.A. Times subscription because their editorial and letters pages are too liberal, with little or no room for conservative opinion. I cancelled USA TODAY because of liberal slant and their betrayal of traditional letter-writers – focusing of blurbs from Facebook and Twitter.

I cancelled my San Bernardino Sun subscription because of liberal letter slant -- half their letters in response to editorial questions of the week -- and too many letters from L.A. County instead of from loyal readers from our San Bernardino County.

And I cancelled my Wall Street Journal subscription because they ignore letters from readers related to government and politics discussed in editorials and commentary, and the honest, independent opinions of letter-writers. I also cancelled my Washington Post and New York Times online.

Fortunately, our local VV Daily Press remains firmly truthful and balanced, focusing on freedom. Of course, I kept that subscription and I also subscribe to NewMax Magazine. My greatest fear for my family is the failure of our government and the direction President Obama has taken against America.

For years, I have felt that my opinions have been of value to readers, and I have had many letters published, which I have consolidated into 5 published volumes of Letters to the Editor: From the Trenches of Democracy, which includes commentary and tips on writing letters. Volume 6 will be published after the 2016 Presidential Election.

Daniel B. Jeffs
Apple Valley

Note: Below is an email to me from the WSJ letters editor, and my response:

From: timothy.lemmer@wsj.com [mailto:timothy.lemmer@wsj.com]
On Behalf Of ltrs, wsj
Sent: Monday, May 02, 2016 9:51 AM
To: Dan Jeffs <directdemocracy@earthlink.net>
Subject: Re: Cancelling newspapers

Mr. Jeffs,
How can you say the Journal ignores letters on government and political issues? That is a slander and is completely wrong. I look at 600 or so letters a day and we run as many as we can fit in the space. I've printed four from you in the past five years.

Timothy Lemmer
Letters Editor
The Wall Street Journal
1211 Sixth Avenue
New York, NY 10036
wsj.ltrs@wsj.com

Mr. Lemmer,
I resent the implications and your condescending attitude, which you displayed the last time I complained to you. Four letters in the last five years is very limited. The only letters on government political issues I've seen for a very long time were the group on the 2016 presidential elections a while back. Too bad, the WSJ is a good newspaper.

Dan Jeffs

Riverside Press Enterprise

April 26, 2016

Letters to the editor:

Scourge of mail theft

My small street of six residences has a group mailbox that was recently pried open and our mail stolen. The theft and vandalism was bad enough but the total lack of interest or action on the part of the Post Office was even worse. I think this problem is much more widespread than we know. The people I spoke with while picking up my mail were from many neighborhoods and some had boxes vandalized multiple times. If the Post Office were a private company, it would be out of business in short order.

John Ray

Woodcrest
(response published)

Riverside Press Enterprise
April 27, 2016

Re: Scourge of mail theft letter
by John Ray
Get a Letter Locker for secure mail
Mr. Ray, I have a suggestion to resolve you and your neighbors mailbox vandalism and mail theft problems. Jayco Industries in Apple Valley manufactures, sells and installs Letter Locker mailboxes, the highest quality and secure mailboxes on the market. Letter Lockers have patented Claw Locks and the boxes cannot be pried open. The boxes are also large enough to store a quantity of mail that remains secure while you are away or on vacation.

Letter Lockers can be ordered via the Jayco Industries and Letter Locker web sites, or you can pick up a box at the manufacturing plant at 21483 Waalew Rd. in Apple Valley, 92307. The Post Office does require group mailboxes, so you might contact your neighbors to arrange for a cluster of six boxes. It's certainly worthwhile looking into. I hope this helps your problem. Our son, Jay Jeffs is the founder and owner of Jayco Industries.

* * * *

Note: This is the unedited letter published in the Washington Times, April 21. 2016.

VV Daily Press
April 27, 2016

2016 American crisis

President Obama has gone too far in accomplishing his promised fundamental transformation of America, managing to intentionally and seriously diminish our domestic and national security, double our national debt, damage our economy, and create deep divisions among our people with the obsessive promotion of his insidious legacy. Indeed, with less than a year to the end of his two terms, Mr. Obama is slamming the pedal to the metal throughout government, America and the world.

And what do we have to look forward to in the 2016 presidential elections? Either Republican Donald Trump, or Democrat Hillary Clinton. Surely, neither of them are promising leaders to the recovery of America. Rather, they are both self-obsessed to the right and left, either too extreme or extremely corrupt leaving voters in a quandary as to what will become of us in a world wrought with terrorism, hate, discontent, social deterioration, economic tribulation, governmental chaos and the threats of world war.

Alas, it's past time for voters to re-evaluate themselves, their lives, their families, their future and the re-established need for our government by the people, for the people, freedom, security, social sanity, and the pursuit of real, not imagined, happiness. To survive, vote your conscience, and hold their feet to the fire of accountability....

The Washington Times
April 22, 2016

Vote your conscience in November

President Obama has gone too far in accomplishing his promised fundamental transformation of America, managing to intentionally and seriously diminish our domestic and national security, double our national debt, damage our economy, and create deep divisions among our people with the obsessive promotion of his insidious legacy. Indeed, with less than a year to the end of his two terms, Mr. Obama is slamming the pedal to the metal throughout government, America and the world.

And what do we have to look forward to in the 2016 presidential elections? Either Republican Donald Trump, or Democrat Hillary Clinton. Surely, neither of them are promising leaders to the recovery of America. Rather, they are both self-obsessed to the right and left, either too extreme or extremely corrupt leaving voters in a quandary as to what will become of us in a world wrought with terrorism, hate, discontent, social deterioration, economic tribulation, governmental chaos and the threats of world war.

Alas, it's past time for voters to re-evaluate themselves, their lives, their families, their future and the re-established need for our government by the people, for the people. To survive, vote your conscience this November -- and hold the candidate's feet to the fire of accountability.

VV Daily Press
April 17, 2016

Real wrongdoers not being punished

Former president Bill Clinton taking on Black Lives Matter about black on black crime, etc. is reminiscent of his romancing the middle during his presidency. For purely political reasons, and to get re-elected, he went along with the Contract with America Republican/ Gingrich Congress in sentencing reform, welfare reform, etc. which were very successful.

However, the $5 billion housing mortgage settlement against Goldman Sachs as being part of the 2008 financial meltdown fails to recognize the real cause, What has been seriously neglected, is that

Clinton forced the housing finance industry to give home loans to unqualified buyers (primarily blacks) who could not afford them. Therefore, Clinton caused the 2008 housing and financial collapse, not Wall Street.

Indeed, the constant call, backed by the liberal media, for executive heads to roll over the financial crisis is wrongheaded. Instead, there should be efforts to punish Bill Clinton, his then hit-team against banks and mortgage lenders, Attorney General Janet Reno, HUD Direct Andrew Cuomo, and Fannie Mae manipulator Franklin Raines should be punished. And, lest it's forgotten, Rep. Barney Frank and Sen. Chris Dodd for perpetuating the fraud.

President Bush attempted to stop the mortgage madness, but his efforts were derailed by Frank, Dodd and Democrats in Congress. Bush attempted to soften the financial blow with TARP and other measures. And, of course, newly-elected President Obama falsely blamed Bush and Wall Street for the costly Clinton/Democrat fiasco.

Alas, the tendency of liberal government and media to punish essentially innocent companies as wrongdoers when they are the real culprits is unconscionable, bad for the economy, bad for business, and worse, bad for the country and our people. President Obama simply perpetuated the recession, exacerbated by two terms of economic lies, abuse and doubling and nation debt.

The Clinton's back in the White House would be wrong. Time for voters to wise-up and get it right. It's a matter of our survival....

Riverside Press Enterprise
April 13, 2016

Taxpayers lose with hefty raise for CSU faculty

Giving in to the demands of the nation's largest public university faculty union in California, giving its members a 10.5 percent raise in salaries to avert a strike is an affront against California taxpayers. Particularly when the Cal State system is nothing more than a finishing school for liberal indoctrination taught in schools throughout the nation.

Surely, aggressive teacher unions are prime examples of why there should be no public employee unions or strikes against taxpayers and the public interest anywhere in the United States, for any reason. It's simply unconscionable and unconstitutional to allow a deleterious ideology to "wag the dog" of government and the American people.

(Original letter)

No public employee unions

Giving in to the demands of the nation's largest public university faculty union in California, giving them a 10.5% raise in salaries to avert a strike, is an affront against California taxpayers. Particularly, when the Cal State system is nothing more than a finishing school for liberal indoctrination in public schools, which is prevalent through-out the nation.

Worse, wagging-the-public-dog of miseducation by the intimi-dation of state teacher unions, the NEA, the federal department of education and the evils of tenure have undermined the minds of America's students, robbing them of their education by manipulating their minds in factories of ignorance for the sake of a liberal ideology is un-American

Surely, aggressive teacher unions are prime examples of why there should be no public employee unions or strikes against taxpayers and the public interest anywhere in the United States for any reason. It's simply unconscionable and unconstitutional to allow a deleterious ideology to wag=the-dog of government and the American people.

Indeed, it is simply divisive, insidious politics and a danger to our children, our domestic and national security our freedom and our future....

VV Daily Press
April 11, 2016

Obama and Pravda

President Obama's speech at the Journalism awards ceremony, telling them that Journalists should hold (Republican) presidential candidates accountable for their actions and policy statements confirms his undue influence over the already liberal news media.

Indeed, President Obama speaks as the acting chairman of the liberal (Putin-controlled Pravda light-like) news media in furthering his corrosive fundamental transformation of the United States America from a Democratic Republic to an authoritarian-style state. No accountability allowed.

Unfortunately, Mr. Obama began his life as one of the last members of the heavy-laden liberal element of the Boomer generation, who infected their children and the next generation in their hostile counter-cultural and political takeover of the safe conservative-American republic as it was founded.

Alas, the Clintons were the first of the Boomer generation, and Obama has been the last and end-all of an insidious revolution, which could end it all for our freedom. Particularly if Hillary Clinton becomes president as the power and greed commander-in-chief.

Clearly, Obama, Clinton and the liberal media have betrayed the Constitution and the First Amendment. Donald Trump is a troubling alternative, but far better than a Clinton-continued calamity....

Riverside Press Enterprise
April 7, 2016

$15 an hour buys a lot of votes

Assessing President Obama and Governor Brown: a bleak 2016?

In assessing the Obama administration's social, political, economic and national security disasters of leading up to and including 2015, and looking forward to the president's final round vs. America, the American people are clearly confused by hope and uncertainty as the chaos of the 2016 Presidential election plays out.

Gov. Brown's insane Propositions and legislators' punishing taxation on businesses, strapping taxpayers with bonds for a totally unnecessary high speed rail, and now the $15 minimum wage have added extreme levels of taxes and burdens upon California business, the people and our economy.

These are calamities for America and California, if voters don't wise up to protect ourselves and our future. Don't cast stupid votes!

VV Daily Press
April 5, 2016

April Fools?

Earlier last month, my wife and I received a vague letter notification from Verizon that Frontier Communications will be taking over our FIOS, Internet and phone services? Early last week we received an undated form letter notification from Frontier Communications President and CEO, Dan McCarthy with "exciting news" indicating that on April 1st, our services would be moved to the Frontier Network in a smooth transition.

Not true for FIOS! The transition began several days before that, and is still going on. Our On Demand services and purchased movies are gone and not available for viewing. Needless to say, we are outraged by the inefficiency. Indeed, we have spent hundreds of dollars on movies, many of which are new releases that should be available.

The Frontier letter advised us to go to "MeetFrontier.com" for a Frontier ID and access. The site is a tangled mess. I attempted to contact Verizon and Frontier by phone with no results. I was "blown-off" by voice recordings from each, to contact the other. Today is April 2nd, and the transition is not complete, Phone, Internet and TV have not been disturbed, but movies are still not available.

Surely, this "April Fools" day was certainly not a joke. It's a betrayal by Verizon FIOS, and gross incompetency by Frontier. I searched the Internet for information on Frontier Communications, but only learned that the company have serious financial problems last year.

Worse, I found that most, if not all newspapers and news media have had nothing to report.

Indeed, we subscribe to USA TODAY, the Wall Street Journal, the Los Angeles Times, the San Bernardino Sun and the Daily Press, and found nothing, including nothing from all of our major online newspaper subscriptions. Alas, one would think that this enormous transition from Verizon FIOS to Frontier Communications that included millions of subscribers from California, Florida and Texas is a big deal. Apparently not.

Hopefully, I speak for most of my fellow disappointed Verizon FIOS customers. Meanwhile, we're waiting, now impatiently, for the business of consumer justice – not here yet!

(Hateful letter and author's response)

VV Daily Press
March 25, 2016

Propaganda vs. reality

Wow! It was a wingnut love fest today, March 24, for the Cranky Old White Men of Apple Valley. All three spewing their vitriol, intolerance, and ignorance on the same editorial page. I really did not read their letters all the way through, since their diatribes are as predictable and trite as all the others they have written. They are a template of the Repugnican (as in Repugnant) propaganda spewed daily by Fox News: President Obama is the worst person in the world who is destroying the USA single-handedly; ObamaCare is the worst government program in the world; all the world's ills can be blamed on the liberals; Repugnicans good, Democrats evil.

The Crankies, you see, are members of the GOP — God's Only People. Only they have the God-given right to rule America. Only their candidates should win. Only their opinions matter, since they possess superior knowledge over all of us who don't agree with them. In other words, they possess no democratic instincts whatsoever.

They are inerrant. It's all about them. We who think differently than they do don't matter.

I am guessing, though, that these three have it made. They never had is so good, but that doesn't stop the gritching and groaning. They love their socialist programs, Social Security and Medicare, even though they paid in a lot less than they will receive. They live in the Fox News twilight zone of balanced government budgets, the end of welfare and food stamps, big concealed weapons and big, high walls on the border.

Boys, why don't you go to the library and educate yourselves. The world doesn't revolve around you. All the modern, progressive things we take for granted — Social Security, 40-hour work week, Medicare, family leave, ban on child labor, unemployment insurance, auto safety, etc. — sprang from liberal, progressive thinking. Your side of the political equation comes up with nothing except tax cuts for the rich, which have just worked wonders, haven't they? Please take off your Fox News-colored glasses and experience reality.

Edward Weinberg
Barstow

VV Daily Press
March 30, 2016

Condescending diatribe

Hesitant to lower myself to a writer's level, I seldom, if ever, engage in personal debates with the left. However his personal attacks are beyond the pale.

His spiteful condescending diatribe against conservative letter-writers is painful evidence of his indoctrination as one of useful idiots of the far left, which is a clear and present danger to our society and America.

Surely, his scurrilous comments about "cranky old white men of Apple Valley" and the "GOP God's Only People" are blatantly racist and bigoted -- unfortunately, expected from the hateful Left.

It's a shame that he doesn't appreciate being published in a conservative, libertarian newspaper.

Indeed, his hypocrisy is the result of a vast infection spread by the un-American discrimination of the intolerant left, which is carried by government, the news media, the education establishment and the entertainment industry.

No conservative speech allowed. Enough said!

Daniel B. Jeffs
Apple Valley

VV Daily Press
March 28, 2016

Valley Voices
Commentary

Supreme Court Injustice
By Daniel Jeffs

Democrats and the liberal news media never let up with their tyrannical intimidation of conservatives to further their insidious agenda against America and the traditional values of the Founders.

Indeed, the Supreme Court has become the focal point of what's wrong with our society, under siege by socialists who are determined to undermine our Constitution and our founding principles.

Clearly, the leaders of the war against America are well-documented in our history, including what was supposed to be the chief safeguard of our Constitution. The Supreme Court of the United States.

Surely, the brutal liberal lynching by Senate Judiciary Sen. Joe Biden against Supreme Court nominees Robert Bork and Clarence Thomas is clear and convincing evidence of authoritarian Democrats against the Constitution.

Certainly, Republican mistakes have been made in the appointments of Supreme Court Justices, John Paul Stevens, Sandra Day

O'Conner, Anthony Kennedy, and Chief Justice John Roberts – not to mention the drastic mistake of Chief Justice Earl Warren by President Eisenhower....

Of course, Democrat presidents Clinton and Obama have ensured the Court's liberal agenda and indifference to Constitutional law with the appointments of justices Ruth Bader Ginsburg, Stephen Breyer, Sonia Sotomayor and Elena Kagan.

Alas, the latest grave injustice is being attempted by President Obama's nomination of Merrick Garland, an Anthony Kennedy-like teetering centrist/socialist to replace the deeply troubling constitutional originalist vacancy left by deceased patriot Justice Antonin Scalia. Yet will still have patriot Justice Samuel Alito.

Sadly, that's the authoritarian liberal way of President Obama's terms of contempt for America, by simply ignoring and circumventing the Constitution. Supreme Court injustice, indeed, like the presidency and government, the Supreme Court problem is systemic. Absolute power in government and on the Court corrupts, absolutely.

We, the American people must correct it, for our survival....
Daniel B. Jeffs is an Apple Valley resident

San Diego Union-Tribune
March 25, 2016

Reaching out to Cuba

Regarding "New Cuba policy a historic smart gamble," March 22.

President Obama's normalization of relations with Castro's brutal Communist regime is nothing more than continuing his blind pursuit of a self-aggrandizing legacy, un-American, and a blatant betrayal of the United States.

Indeed, America's gravest mistake was failing to prevent Fidel Castro's Communist aggression to take over Cuba. Clearly, the mistake was exacerbated by failing to overthrow Castro after the Russian-backed Cuban missile crisis.

Coupled with the military failure to take out Castro in the Cuban patriot Bay of Pigs effort, allowing Castro to rule on and spread Communism in South America and beyond, was reprehensible.

Surely, President Obama's actions are too close and dangerous to our national security. The solution, of course, is to squeeze the Castro regime out of existence and free the Cuban people to have a democratic republic. Regime change is the answer....

San Bernardino Sun
March 24, 2016

Donald Trump destroying the Republican Party

Self-consumed commercial hustler Donald Trump has played upon conservative anger against the corrosive liberal Democrat Party establishment by running for president in the 2016 election, which handed the Democrats the opportunity to create the perfect storm against him and the Republican Party.

And the liberal Democrat cartel of government, news media and education are doing it. This is not politics as usual. It is in fact a looming calamity (an event that causes great harm and suffering) for America.

Unacceptable! Particularly in this era of domestic and national security peril. Vote for survival.

(Note: Trump, Clinton and Obama are all cut from the same self-absorbed cloth. The striking difference is, Trump is productive.)

VV Daily Press
March 24, 2016

Trump calamity

Self-consumed commercial hustler Donald Trump has played upon conservative anger against the corrosive liberal Democrat Party establishment by running for president in the 2016 election, which handed the Democrats the opportunity to create the perfect storm against him and the Republican Party.

And the liberal Democrat cartel of government, news media and education are doing it. This is not politics as usual. It is in fact a looming calamity (an event that causes great harm and suffering) for America.

Unacceptable! Particularly in this era of domestic and national security peril. Vote for survival.

(Note: Trump, Clinton and Obama are all cut from the same self-absorbed cloth. The striking difference is, Trump is productive.)

The Washington Times
March 23, 2016

Greatest threat: Leftist ideology

Since the eras of Franklin D. Roosevelt, Woodrow Wilson and Teddy Roosevelt, the insidious liberal Democrat ideology has tightened its iron grip on America by infecting our government, our schools, our news media and the entertainment industry. All of this has had an extensive influence over our society.

Indeed, if it were not for people who hold fast to conservative Republican and libertarian constitutional principles, freedoms, moral values and religion, our nation and our future would be lost forever to liberal indoctrination.

The 2016 presidential election run-up has been a brutal display of the battle between good and evil, exacerbated by two terms of the insidious Obama administration, starring Republican Donald Trump, and Democrats Hillary Clinton and Sen. Bernie Sanders of Vermont.

Unfortunately, pathological narcissist billionaire Donald Trump is a political anomaly, a gift to Democrats intent on destroying the Republicans. He is playing into their insidious ideology.

Fortunately, Republican candidates such as Ohio Gov. John Kasich and Sen. Ted Cruz of Texas have the wherewithal to beat Mr. Trump, Mrs. Clinton and Mr. Sanders. That is, if the Republican Party gets its act together and works to dismantle the greatest threat to our country: Liberal Democrat ideology....

VV Daily Press
March 23, 2016

Supreme Court Injustice

Democrats and the liberal news media never let up with their tyrannical intimidation of conservatives to further their insidious agenda against America and the traditional values of the Founders.

Indeed, the Supreme Court has become the focal point of what's wrong with our society, under siege by socialists who are determined to undermine our Constitution and our founding principles.

Clearly, the leaders of the war against America are well-documented in our history, including what was supposed to be the chief safeguard of our Constitution. The Supreme Court of the United States.

Surely, the brutal liberal lynching by Senate Judiciary Sen. Joe Biden against Supreme Court nominees Robert Bork and Clarence Thomas is clear and convincing evidence of authoritarian Democrats against the Constitution.

Certainly, Republican mistakes have been made in the appointments of Supreme Court Justices, John Paul Stevens, Sandra Day O'Conner, Anthony Kennedy, and Chief Justice John Roberts – not to mention the drastic mistake of Chief Justice Earl Warren by President Eisenhower....

Of course, Democrat presidents Clinton and Obama have ensured the Court's liberal agenda and indifference to Constitutional law with the appointments of justices Ruth Bader Ginsburg, Stephen Breyer, Sonia Sotomayor and Elena Kagan.

Alas, the latest grave injustice is being attempted by President Obama's nomination of Merrick Garland, an Anthony Kennedy-like teetering centrist/socialist to replace the deeply troubling constitutional originalist vacancy left by deceased patriot Justice Antonin Scalia. Yet will still have patriot Justice Samuel Alito.

Sadly, that's the authoritarian liberal way of President Obama's terms of contempt for America, by simply ignoring and circumventing the Constitution. Supreme Court injustice, indeed, like the presidency and government, the Supreme Court problem is systemic. Absolute power in government and on the Court corrupts, absolutely.

We, the American people must correct it, for our survival....

VV Daily Press
March 16, 2016

Election insanity 2016

When Donald Trump announced his Republican bid for president, he seized the stage as ringmaster in the greatest show of political insanity on earth, turning the Republican race into upside down side-shows.

On the Democrat side, corrupt pathological narcissist candidate Hillary Clinton seized upon her coronation role as the first woman president, complicated by the insanity of grumpy old man socialist Bernie Sanders.

Of course, all the insanity is being exacerbated by biased news media sensationalism. Hopefully, voters will wise-up enough to elect a president who will lead us out of the insane darkness into the light of America's survival.

Indeed, Ohio Gov. John Kasich is the only grounded, qualified candidate with the character, integrity and deeply proven federal and state government experience to pull our country together against government self-destruction, economic ruin and terrorism.

VV Daily Press
March 7, 2016

The next president

Re: "GOP has more to lose than gain" … Absolutely. Who will be elected president in 2016?

Considering the probable nominees, it doesn't look good for America. Clinton or Trump? No!

Unfortunately, too may clueless and indoctrinated voters influenced by biased media will go along with lemming voter-assisted suicide, one way or the other. Why? It already happened with two-term President Obama: Social, political, economic, domestic and national security disaster.

Worse, the state of the Republican Party, Democrat Party and outsiders in the presidential election have created a Trump-driven, ringmaster-cheapened political circus with ugly side-shows, making it painfully clear that America is steeped in election trouble.

The news media, of course, are exacerbating the dilemma. Surely, It's time for voters to get our act together and promote real democracy wherein we decide, not the personal power hungry narcissistic fools running our country into the ground....

Sen. Rubio or Sen. Cruz are OK alternatives, particularly against a Corrupt Hillary Clinton or a grumpy old socialist, Bernie Sanders.

However, Ohio Gov. John Kasich is the only grounded, qualified candidate with the character, integrity and deeply proven federal and state government experience to pull our country together against government self-destruction, economic ruin and terrorism.

Question is, can exasperated Republicans make the smart move to expel Trump from the nominations and make the right move? Our future will depend upon it.

Riverside Press-Enterprise
March 3, 2016

Kasich our last chance

Who will be elected president in 2016? Considering the probable nominees, it doesn't look good for America. Clinton or Trump? No!

Unfortunately, too may clueless and indoctrinated voters influenced by biased media will go along with lemming voter-assisted suicide. Why? It already happened with two-term President Obama: Social, political, economic, domestic and national security disasters.

Worse, the state of the Republican Party, Democrat Party and outsiders in the presidential election have created a Trump-driven, ringmaster-cheapened political circus with ugly side-shows, making it painfully clear that America is steeped in election trouble.

The news media, of course, are exacerbating the dilemma. It's time for voters to get our act together and promote real democracy wherein we decide -- not the personal power-hungry narcissistic fools running our country into the ground....

Sen. Rubio or Sen. Cruz are OK alternatives, particularly against Corrupt Hillary Clinton or socialist Bernie Sanders.

However, Ohio Gov. John Kasich is the only grounded, qualified candidate with the character, integrity and deeply proven federal and state government experience to pull our country together against government self-destruction, economic ruin and terrorism.

VV Daily Press
February 29, 2016

Apple vs. America

Apple's refusal to co-operate with the FBI regarding the encrypted phone records of the San Bernardino, CA terrorists is simply un-patriotic and un-American.

Particularly, in the insidious climate of national security failures created by President Obama's dereliction of duty over the past seven years of fundamentally and dangerously transforming America.

Surely, Apple and all American tech companies should be working hard with our domestic and national security officials to prevent terrorist attacks, and to attack terrorists working to hack and attack us, our government, businesses, power grids and our freedom.

Indeed, President Obama is directly responsible for the rise and proliferation of al-Qaeda, ISIS and terrorism in the Middle-East,

America and throughout the world – and the criminal invasion across our borders -- which are tantamount to treason.

Clearly, if it were not for this climate of treason, there would have been no post-2008 traitors such as the terrorist attacks in America at Fort Hood, Texas, San Bernardino – and no traitors such as Manning and Snowden – or the aggression of Russia, North Korea and China – or peace with Communist Cuba.

Alas, the liberal media should be ashamed for supporting the treasonous, as should Hollywood for supporting the government-caused fall of the economy, and Oliver Stone for his un-American activities and for glorifying Traitor Edward Snowden.

Enough! Voters must wise-up and elect a patriotic Republican president and Congress in the 2016 elections. For our survival....

Riverside Press Enterprise
February 25, 2016

Obama's Gitmo legacy

Re: "Obama's Guantanamo plan hits wall of opposition" [Front page, Feb. 24]:

President Obama doesn't miss a beat in orchestrating his insidious legacy of fundamentally transforming America.

Indeed, he is determined to release more terrorists from Guantanamo back into rejoining the terrorist jihad against America and the West, and transferring the remaining terrorists to federal prisons – increasing the danger to our people.

Of course, if the Congress does not approve Mr. Obama's proposed actions to close Guantanamo, he will surely circumvent the Congress and the Constitution again with his all-too-frequent monarchial executive actions.

Edited out: [Surely, President Obama intends to give Guantanamo back to Communist Cuba to complete reconciliation with the insidious Castro regime.]

VV Daily Press
February 22, 2016

President 2016

The New Hampshire primary election launched the proving grounds of a Hillary Clinton and Bernie Sanders fight over who is going to best continue and expand on President "Barwreck" Obama's corrosive policies -- and a battle for the Republican spirit of American recovery.

Indeed, through the campaign chaos, indoctrinated Democrats must choose between a Hillary Clinton crook and a Bernie Sanders socialist. And reminiscent Republicans must choose between a sword, shield and chariot charging Donald Trump -- and a winner in wisdom.

Surely, the best outcome would be an honest Republican president and Congress who stimulate true American culture, values and character among the people, similar to how a "We're looking out for you" Bill O'Reilly does.

And that's the truth!

San Diego Union-Tribune
February 18, 2016

Readers weigh in on replacing Justice Scalia

President Obama's assertion that he is going to nominate an undisputable replacement for Supreme Court Justice Antonin Scalia is simply another example of his monarchial arrogance.

Indeed, he should know better, however, considering his history of unlawful executive orders and edicts circumventing the Congress and the Constitution, Mr. Obama is incapable of deviating from his insidious legacy of fundamentally transforming America.

Alas, President Obama can't help himself.

Riverside Press Enterprise
February 16, 2016

Scalia was a defender of our ideals

The untimely death of Supreme Court Justice Antonin Scalia is a great loss to the enforcement of and defense of the original intent and interpretation of the U.S. Constitution, our founding document. Indeed, he was a great jurist and true American.

Unfortunately, President Obama announced that he would nominate a successor to Justice Scalia rather than leaving the nomination to the next president to be elected this year.

Of course, he wrongfully intends to nominate a justice who would carry out his legacy of fundamentally transforming America to a legacy of tearing down our Republic and our future of freedom, as he continues to circumvent the Congress and the Constitution with executive orders and monarchial edicts, unabated.

Clearly, the Republican Senate must reject Mr. Obama's nomination to the court. Our country has suffered enough under his administration, seriously damaging our domestic and national security.

Again, our only hope is to elect a strong conservative president such as Sen. Marco Rubio, maintain a Republican Congress and replace the leading conservative voice on the Court with a constitutionalist like Justice Scalia.

VV Daily Press
February 16, 2016

Valley Voices (commentary)
Revolting development scenarios
By Daniel B. Jeffs

The rise of uncivilized Islamic assaults on civilization in the world, have been exacerbated by the rise of uncivilized technology resulting in superficial societies of selfish interests, social aggression, political tyranny, economic stress and extremes – particularly in America.

Indeed, America -- the model and historical leader of peace and freedom in the world -- has been severely undermined by the post-WWII cultural revolution resulting in tearing down our established institutions, corrupting our society and diminishing our freedoms.

Clearly, the revolting developments have been caused by social, political and economic extremists from the 1960's and 70's, who spawned countercultural hate and decay in society and government, leaving America vulnerable to attack by enemies from within and the outside.

Which leads us the revolting political developments of now and how we got here. Alas, most Democrats have made a costly mess of things, and most Republicans have been less than efficient in cleaning it up. The best of both have been Kennedy and Reagan. The worst: Carter, Clinton and Obama.

Surely, the best outcome for the 2016 presidential election would be either Rubio, Kasich, Christie or Fiorina. The worst would be Hillary Clinton or Bernie Sanders, with Barack Obama on the Supreme Court. The elephant in the room isn't really an elephant. He's certainly not a Trump card. He's a dangerous anomaly.

Presidential race to oblivion?

It's still the economy, stupid is not Hillary Clinton's truth any more than it was in 1992, when Bill Clinton schemed his way into the presidency, then undermined the economy by causing the unaffordable housing and financial collapse of 2008.

Indeed, the counter cultural revolution and decades of extremist and socialist indoctrination by the miseducation and media cartel came to fruition with the 2008 election of Barack Obama, humiliating John McCain and the bumbling Republican Party, and assigning Hillary Clinton to dismantle foreign policy and escalate terrorism.

Now, the 2016 presidential race to America's oblivion is on again, with corruption-in-her-heart and fire-in-her-eyes Hillary Clinton leading, challenged by the cranky old socialist Bernie Sanders and his wild-young indoctrinated crowd of supporters.

Of course, they're being chased by a narrowing herd of patriotic Republicans, stampeded by wheeler-dealer Donald Trump, and struggling to gain traction with Cruz, Rubio, Carson, Christie and Kasich – with a Bush in the background.

Alas, the liberal media curse is the venomous snake in the grass that will frighten the voter multitude all the way through to the poisoned finish line. Hopefully, the American voters will be concerned enough to find the antidote and a way back to the strong tradition of who we are: Home of the brave and land of the free.

Question is, who will it be? First woman,? first Hispanic? or who? -- I vote for Kasich/Fiorina, for political sanity.

Daniel B. Jeffs is an Apple Valley resident and retired law enforcement officer who served on two San Bernardino County Grand Juries.

* * * *

The same SUN letter in the Daily Press with the original title:

VV Daily Press
February 14, 2016

Other people's money

President Obama is on the tax tyranny against self-reliance express again by proposing an oil tax of $10 per barrel that will increase gasoline, diesel and heating oil prices in his climate change hoax carbon attacks on energy, which will drive up the cost of living.

Indeed, that doesn't matter to seizing other people's money liberals, California Governor Brown included. Worse, if either socialist Senator Bernie Sanders or the corrupt Hillary Clinton should be elected president, the road to ruin would continue unabated.

What we need from the 2016 presidential elections is a strong conservative president and Congress to rescue our superficial society of social aggression, political vitriol, selfish interests and extremes from the grip of decades of inept, overbearing government and liberal indoctrination.

It's a dire matter of America's survival.

San Bernardino Sun
February 12, 2016

Obama's tax tyranny

Re: "Obama sends Congress record $4.1 trillion 2017 federal budget" (Feb. 9):

President Obama is on the tax tyranny against self-reliance express again by proposing an oil tax of $10 per barrel that will increase gasoline, diesel and heating oil prices in his climate change hoax carbon attacks on energy, which will drive up the cost of living.

Indeed, that doesn't matter to seizing other people's money liberals, California Governor Brown included. Worse, if either socialist Senator Bernie Sanders or the corrupt Hillary Clinton should be elected president, the road to ruin would continue unabated.

What we need from the 2016 presidential elections is a strong conservative president and Congress to rescue our superficial society of social aggression, political vitriol, selfish interests and extremes from the grip of decades of inept, overbearing government and liberal indoctrination.

It's a dire matter of America's survival.

VV Daily Press
February 8, 2016

Brown's attack on California

Governor Brown is so wrapped-up in himself as the only real governor of California, that he fanaticizes about holding the office until his last breath. However, when and if reality sets in, the state will realize that he has been little more than a political hustler whose Prop. 30 taxed the lives, and Prop. 47 endangered the lives of the people of the state. Now he has another prison initiative to release even criminals to prey on the people.

Indeed, Gov. Jerry has been the miserable master of California's punishing taxes, implementing anti-economy Prop. 32 regulations, the miseducation money pit, sanctuary state of crime, leaking rainy day surpluses, drought neglect, and the San Francisco to Los Angeles bullet train wreck. Clearly, Mr. Brown now wants his $68 billion-times-two-toy train to start in Northern California instead of Southern so he can play with it first.

All at taxpayers' expense and security, of course. For that is the languishing lament of liberal state politics – and what a longtime diminishing development it has been. Alas, rather than suffering in silence, it's time to for voters to wise-up and make changes to survive and prosper – for a change....

VV Daily Press
February 1, 2016

Brown's bullet train wreck

Governor Brown is so wrapped-up in himself as the only real governor of California, that he fanaticizes about holding the office until his last breath. However, when and if reality sets in, the state will realize that he has been little more than a political hustler whose Prop. 30 taxed the lives, and Prop. 47 endangered the lives of the people of the state.

Indeed, Gov. Jerry has been the miserable master of California's miseducation money pit, sanctuary state of crime, leaking rainy day surpluses, drought neglect, and the San Francisco to Los Angeles bullet train wreck. Clearly, Mr. Brown now wants his $68 billion-times-two-toy train to start in Northern California instead of Southern so he can play with it first.

All at taxpayers' expense, of course. For that is the languishing lament of liberal state politics – and what a longtime diminishing development it has been. Alas, it's time to for voters to wise-up and make changes to survive – for a change....

(Revised letter sent)
Gov. Brown's attack on California

Governor Brown is so wrapped-up in himself as the only real governor of California, that he fanaticizes about holding the office until his last breath. However, when and if reality sets in, the state will realize that he has been little more than a political hustler whose Prop. 30 taxed the lives, and Prop. 47 endangered the lives of the people of the state. Now he has another prison initiative to release even criminals to prey on the people.

Indeed, Gov. Jerry has been the miserable master of California's punishing taxes, implementing anti-economy Prop. 32 regulations, the miseducation money pit, sanctuary state of crime, leaking rainy day surpluses, drought neglect, and the San Francisco to Los Angeles bullet train wreck. Clearly, Mr. Brown now wants his $68 billion-times-two-toy train to start in Northern California instead of Southern so he can play with it first.

All at taxpayers' expense and security, of course. For that is the languishing lament of liberal state politics – and what a longtime diminishing development it has been. Alas, rather than suffering in silence, it's time to for voters to wise-up and make changes to survive and prosper – for a change….

VV Daily Press
January 26, 2016

Obama's Iran scam

President Obama and Secretary of State Kerry have taken a giant step backward in giving the terrorist state of Iran everything they want, with nothing in return but seriously reducing our national security. Indeed, our naval patrol boats unintentionally straying into Iranian waters gave the president exactly what he needed to complete the national security nightmare deal with Iran.

Clearly, it wasn't enough sucking-up to Iran for releasing our humiliated sailors. No, President Obama and his Secretary of State stooge Kerry seized the moment, gave away the farm and bowed-down to terrorist Iran in the worst of ways, by making another unbalanced exchange for U.S. prisoners, removing all sanctions, releasing $billions in funds, and finalizing the phony nuclear deal.

Which, of course, puts Israel, America and the world in ever-greater danger -- leaves our long-held FBI agent hostage in Iran -- and by releasing Guantanamo terrorists, Mr. Obama continues to exacerbate the damage to our overall national security. Clearly, coupled with laying America bare to terrorism, President "Osama" Obama's insidious pursuit of his warped legacy is simply insane....

Alas, January 2017 can't come soon enough, hopefully without the scurrilous corruption of Clinton....

VV Daily Press
January 20, 2016

Public betrayal in Hollywood

Black activists hardly have room to complain about being snubbed by white dominated Hollywood awards time. Particularly, when black movies have increased over the past few years. Indeed, *Concussion* was black dominated because sports are black dominated. And *Straight outta Compton* was a success, even though irresponsible in depicting angry black gangster rap, which is damaging to young people and society – yet very popular so-called music that is frequently used in movies. Surely, it must be noted that blacks are over-represented in television, commercials and many movies.

The *Big Short* incompletely and irresponsibly depicts Wall Street greed as the culprit in the 2008 housing and financial crash, when in fact, it was President Clinton and his administration who caused the collapse by intimidating banks and mortgage lenders into giving home loans to unqualified buyers to push his affordable housing agenda. Wall Street simply did the best they could in reaction to being faced with disaster.

Spotlight incompletely and irresponsibly depicts the child molestation in the Catholic clergy, but fails to portray why it happened: A massive move by gay pedophiles into Catholic seminaries during the 1970's and 1980's, wherein, as Catholic priests, they would have an unlimited supply of altar-boy victims to prey upon. The church was simply the overwhelmed by the predators and struggled to deal with it.

Alas, Hollywood certainly falls short in depicting truth, overdone with violence, lacking in social responsibility, and long on shamelessly celebrating themselves....

(Revised last paragraph sent later)
Public betrayal in Hollywood (revised)

Black activists hardly have room to complain about being snubbed by white dominated Hollywood awards time. Particularly, when black movies have increased over the past few years. Indeed, *Concussion* was black dominated because sports are black dominated. And *Straight outta Compton* was a success, even though irresponsible in depicting angry black gangster rap, which is damaging to young people and society – yet very popular so-called music that is frequently used in movies. Surely, it must be noted that blacks are over-represented in television, commercials and many movies.

The *Big Short* incompletely and irresponsibly depicts Wall Street greed as the culprit in the 2008 housing and financial crash, when in fact, it was President Clinton and his administration who caused the collapse by intimidating banks and mortgage lenders into giving home loans to unqualified buyers to push his affordable housing agenda. Wall Street simply did the best they could in reaction to being faced with disaster.

Spotlight incompletely and irresponsibly depicts the child molestation in the Catholic clergy, but fails to portray why it happened: A massive move by gay pedophiles into Catholic seminaries during the 1970's and 1980's, wherein, as Catholic priests, they would have an unlimited supply of altar-boy victims to prey upon. The church was simply the overwhelmed by the predators and struggled to deal with it.

Alas, Hollywood certainly falls short in depicting truth, overdone with violence, lacking in social responsibility, and long on shamelessly celebrating themselves, with few exceptions. Fortunately, *Joy*, the true story of Joy Mangano and her HSN mop, played by Jennifer Lawrence, recognizes true success with social redeeming value and worthy of reward for both Joy's achievements....

San Diego Union-Tribune
January 18, 2016

Sean Penn should be ashamed of his actions

Sean Penn is at least a three-strike traitor and should be in jail or worse. Over time, he has aided and comforted our enemies, Saddam Hussein, Hugo Chavez, and now the current infamous drug lord -- with impunity -- simply because he's a so-called talented Hollywood actor.

Problem is, he has been an arrogant, un-American bad actor who, unfortunately, represents the infected, self-absorbed arrogance of Hollywood's sick manipulation of America's movie-going mind -- Kick-start the Golden Globes and the warped deceit of the mindless award season...

VV Daily Press
January 17, 2016

Sean Penn is a traitor

Sean Penn is at least a three-strike traitor and should be in jail or worse. Over time, he has aided and comforted our enemies, Saddam Hussein, Hugo Chavez, and now the current infamous drug lord -- with impunity -- simply because he's a so-called talented Hollywood actor.

Problem is, he has been an arrogant, un-American bad actor who, unfortunately, represents the infected, self-absorbed arrogance of Hollywood's sick manipulation of America's movie-going mind -- Kick-start the Golden Globes and the warped deceit of the mindless award season...

San Bernardino Sun
January 17, 2016

State of union a mess under President Obama

Under the painful, indefensible administration of President Obama – backed by the irresponsible liberal media -- the state of the union has gone from disheveled to seriously fractured and dangerous, hopefully not beyond repair.

The solution: We, the American people, and our elected representatives must get our collective act together, recover from the destructive Obama era and move up to social, political and economic strength, real security and prosperity – the way America is meant to be....

Unfortunately, I am somewhat of a voice in the wilderness, relentlessly doing my best to save our precious nation for the sake of my family, my community, state and country by writing traditional letters to the editor in sea of technology. And so it goes, as long as tangible print news media survives....

Riverside Press-Enterprise
January 14, 2016

Obama's state of disunion salvageable

Under the painful, indefensible administration of President Obama – backed by the irresponsible liberal media -- the state of the union has gone from disheveled to seriously fractured and dangerous, but hopefully not beyond repair.

The solution: We, the American people, and our elected representatives must get our collective act together, recover from the destructive Obama era and move up to social, political and economic strength, real security and prosperity – the way America is meant to be.

Unfortunately, I am somewhat of a voice in the wilderness, relentlessly doing my best to save our precious nation for the sake of my family, my community, state and country by writing traditional letters to the editor in sea of technology.

And so it goes, as long as tangible print news media survives.

VV Daily Press
January 11, 2016

Obama's chaos 2016

President Obama's latest unconstitutional executive orders against gun owners and the Second Amendment comes as no surprise. Clearly, Mr. Obama's staged phony tears over mass murders of children were certainly lacking when he conveniently stopped to meet with families of the victims of the San Bernardino terrorist attack, while on his way to an extended vacation in Hawaii.

Surely, his legacy-building history of unlawful executive orders and edicts have been tantamount to treason. Indeed, President Obama has been on a campaign of creating chaos in America since he took office in 2008, which is consistent with Saul Alinsky's socialist Rules for Radicals, which Hillary Clinton ascribed to in her college thesis. Certainly, they have both betrayed America's national security time after time in dealing with Islamic terrorism

What America must realize is that the Middle East has been in a war of Sunni vs. Shiite tribal savagery for centuries, which is now coming to a head between the Saudi Sunni and Iranian Shia. Lest we forget, we backed Sunni Saddam Hussein when he went to war with Iranian Shia and only took him on when he invaded Kuwait.

Then it all went under because Iran exploited Iraq and the nation building didn't work. Extreme Islamists like al-Qaeda and ISIS simply exacerbates everything against their common infidel enemies, America and the West. Thus we're caught in the middle of the war of savages. Meanwhile we must elect a strong Republican president and Congress, vigorously defend ourselves at all costs, and hope the Islamic terrorists destroy themselves.

VV Daily Press
January 8, 2016

Clinton election would be suicide

We are the American people!

President Obama is a rogue, lawless president, blatantly abusing his executive power, circumventing the Constitution, and contaminating most, if not all, departments of our government -- primarily the DOD, DOJ, EPA, FCC, Homeland Security and the Bureau of Prisons -- which have severely weakened our domestic and national security.

And that, for lack of a better term -- exacerbating the terrorist threat in an era of escalating terrorism -- is recklessly un-American, tantamount to treason.

Indeed, replacing President Obama with Hillary Clinton in the 2016 election would be voter-assisted suicide for our nation.

Therefore, our duty as voters is to elect a highly qualified Republican patriotic dynamic duo from the field of candidates: Sen. Rubio, Gov. Christie, Gov. Kasich and Carly Fiorina as president and vice president to save and recover the United States of America, as intended by our Founders....

Regardless, we will have a Merry Christmas and a Happy New year of determination, simply because we are the American people....

VV Daily Press
January 1, 2016

Presidential candidates

Donald Trump is loose cannon, exploiting American angst, oblivious to Putin's aggression.

Hillary Clinton and President Obama are the team who disassembled the Middle East, abandoned Israel, the Ukraine, NATO and surrendered to terrorism.

Indeed, Obama reduced our nuclear power 90 percent from Reagan's 15,000 warheads to 1,500, while making a bad deal allowing Iran to become a nuclear weapons power, assisted by Putin, leading to the potential of nuclear war.

Clearly, America has reached critical mass, and the 2016 Presidential election is vital to our survival, meaning the direction of leadership must be turned around. But not by a dangerous Donald Trump or a corrupt Hillary Clinton.

Which leaves the right choices against terrorism and for the economy to the voters -- who must elect a presidential team such as Rubio, Fiorina, Cruz, Kasich, Christie and Huckabee -- or any dynamic duo thereof -- including a draft of Romney -- to lead us to safety, security and prosperity.

And a Congress to aggressively represent the best interests of the American people, instead of their own selfish interests....

2015 Letters

The Washington Times
December 28, 2015

In 2016, vote for strength, prosperity

Donald Trump is loose cannon, exploiting American angst, and he is oblivious to Russian President Putin's aggression. Hillary Rodham Clinton and President Obama are the team that disassembled the Middle East and abandoned Israel, Ukraine and NATO, while surrendering to terrorism.

Indeed, Mr. Obama reduced our nuclear power by 90 percent(from Ronald Reagan's 15,000 warheads we are now at 1,500) while making a bad deal that will allow Iran to become a nuclear-weapons power assisted by Putin. This will lead to the potential of nuclear war.

Clearly, America has reached critical mass, and the 2016 Presidential election is vital to our survival. The direction of leadership must be turned around, but not by a dangerous Donald Trump or a corrupt Hillary Clinton.

That leaves the right choices against terrorism and for the economy to the voters, who must elect a presidential team from candidates such as Marco Rubio, Carly Fiorina, Ted Cruz, John Kasich, Chris Christie and Mike Huckabee to lead us to safety, security and prosperity.

We also need a Congress that will aggressively represent the best interests of the American people rather than its own selfish interests....

San Bernardino Sun
December 27, 2015

Proud of police response to SB attack

As a San Bernardino County resident and retired law enforcement officer with 41 years of service with the Los Angeles County and San Bernardino County Sheriff's Departments and the criminal justice system, I am proud of the immediate and courageous response of San Bernardino Police Department to the terrorist attack killing 14 people, injuring 21. And for the rapid follow-up investigation resulting in the deaths of the two terrorists.

I am also grateful for the other law enforcement agencies who assisted in the response, and for the intense, ongoing FBI investigation. However, I am deeply concerned for my family and fellow citizens.

Indeed, the San Bernardino terrorist attack highlights President Obama's feckless lack of an aggressive plan against terrorism. In the aftermath of the San Bernardino massacre, President Obama's speech to the country was little more than meaningless babble masking the fact that he wants to disarm Americans more than prevailing against terrorism.

The Obama administration has grossly failed America's national and domestic security by reducing our military strength, allowing the proliferation of ISIS, not enforcing border security and conducting an unjust war against our police, diminishing our domestic security.

VV Daily Press
December 27, 2015

Obama's legacy

President Obama is simply a phony president, deceiving the American people during his entire time in office, from Obamacare to global warming, from social engineering to the economy, from his limp responses to Russia's aggression to being aloof to fighting terrorism.

Indeed, Mr. Obama's meeting with the families of the San Bernardino terror victims is a matter indifference and convenience, little more than a pit stop on his way to a family vacation in Hawaii, all the while being obsessed by finishing his legacy.

Worse, our nation will be in unnecessary peril until he leaves office. Coupled with the 90's corrosive counterculture Clinton administration, President Obama's cultural abscess has been exacerbated by social divisions, abdicating his duty to domestic and national security.

All, while being oblivious to our fearful nation, steeped in uncertainty....

VV Daily Press
December 22, 2015

Trump and the GOP

Donald Trump is political suicide for the Republican Party.

Following Donald Trump's rise as a potential Republican nominee for the 2016 presidential election has gone from fresh conservative vigor to the inescapable conclusion that Trump as the Republican nominee would amount to political suicide for the Republican Party with dire consequences for our nation.

Indeed, it is certainly understandable that President Obama's abuse of power and his feckless leadership have had a corrosive effect on America's social, political and economic health, exacerbated by his dangerous irresponsibility in dealing with the growing terrorist threats to our national and domestic security.

However, Donald Trump -- the extreme antithesis to President Obama -- is not the answer. Though Trump talks tough and says what he knows his growing followers want to hear, he simply doesn't have the temperament or the character to safely and responsibly lead our country.

Clearly, a president Trump would throw fuel on the fires of terrorism against America.

Instead, conservative, moderates and independents should support candidates such as a team of Sen. Marco Rubio and Carly Fiorina for strong, clearheaded leadership to support and defend our Constitution against all enemies, foreign and domestic -- and to protect the American people.

Surely, the alternative of a president Hillary Clinton is an unacceptable risk. The cynical questions is, there might be a Trump-Ross Perot deception-effect in play, which would hand the presidency to Hillary whether Trump is the Republican nominee or not....

San Diego Union-Tribune
December 18, 2015

Trump's success speaks to the nation's angst

Donald Trump's rise as a potential Republican nominee for the 2016 presidential election has gone from fresh conservative vigor to the inescapable conclusion that Trump as the Republican nominee would amount to political suicide for the Republican Party with dire consequences for our nation.

Though Trump talks tough and says what he knows his growing followers want to hear, he simply doesn't have the temperament or the character to safely and responsibly lead our country.

Instead, conservative, moderates and independents should support candidates such as a team of Sen. Marco Rubio and Carly Fiorina.

Better yet, Republican delegates should draft 2012 candidate Mitt Romney at the 2016 convention, for strong, clearheaded leadership.

VV Daily Press
December 18, 2015

Obama's lack of a plan

As a San Bernardino County resident and retired law enforcement officer with 41 years of service with the Los Angeles County and San Bernardino County Sheriff's Departments and the criminal justice system, I am proud of the immediate and courageous response of San Bernardino Police Department to the terrorist attack and massacre of 14 people – injuring 21 others – who were gathered at a County building in the City.

And for the rapid follow-up investigation resulting in the deaths of the two terrorists. I am also grateful for the other law enforcement agencies who assisted in the response, and for the intense, ongoing FBI investigation.

However, I am deeply concerned for my family and fellow citizens. Indeed, the San Bernardino terrorist attack highlights President Obama's feckless lack of an aggressive plan against terrorism. Indeed, in the aftermath of the San Bernardino massacre, President Obama's speech to the country was little more than meaningless babble masking the fact that he wants to disarm Americans more than prevailing against terrorism.

Clearly, American citizens are arming themselves for defense against criminals and terrorists, and for good reasons. The Obama administration has grossly failed America's national and domestic security by reducing our military strength, allowing the proliferation of ISIS, not enforcing border security and the unchecked flow of illegal aliens including criminals and drugs – and conducting an unjust war against our police, diminishing our domestic security.

Hopefully, the next president will be a real commander in chief rather than a dangerous imposter who put his ideology above our safety, our society, our economy and the future of America.

Riverside Press Enterprise
December 16, 1025

Need for a different kind of climate change

Dwarfing his costly Obamacare failure, President Obama spearheaded his legacy-seeking U.N. conference on climate change in Paris, resulting in a worldwide agreement to avert the worst effects of global warming by shifting economies to cleaner energy sources.

Sadly, the economy-busting climate change deception simply adds to the dangerously corrosive, decades-long social, political and economic climate change in America caused by liberal government, the miseducation establishment and media.

Alas, what America really needs is a reverse climate change -- of good and against evil -- with the strength of determined leadership and limited government. It's a matter of our survival.

(Original letter)

Deadly climate change deception

Dwarfing his costly Obamacare failure, President Obama spearheaded his legacy-seeking UN conference in Paris on Climate Change resulting in a worldwide agreement to avert the worst effects of global warming by shifting economies to cleaner energy sources to reduce greenhouse gas emissions.

However, beginning with Al Gore's Inconvenient Truth global warming deception backed by climate alarmist scientists, the campaign against greenhouse gases went into overdrive, exacerbated by reckless legislative actions highlighted in California by conference attendee, former Gov. Schwarzenegger's punishing AB 32 carbon taxes.

Indeed, Ca. Gov. Brown gave a speech at the Paris conference, followed by a scene outside the center, singing along with Barry McGuire's 1965 song, *"We're on the eve of destruction"* as his legacy-seeking anthem to take drastic actions justifying his radical political moves by slashing oil consumption and sounding false alarms against drought, disasters and terrorism. And, of course, L.A. Mayor

Garcetti attended the conference and jumped on the environmentalist bandwagon.

Sadly, the delirious economy-busting climate change deception simply adds to the dangerously corrosive decades-long social, political and economic climate change in America caused by liberal government, the miseducation establishment and media bent on social, political and economic suicide.

Clearly evidenced by tyrannical laws and taxes, indoctrination of students robbing them of a real education --the Clinton-government-caused 2008 housing and financial meltdown -- President Obama's feckless foreign policy and border enforcement resulting the proliferation of terrorism, illegal alien criminals, gangs and drugs -- and the collapse of our national and domestic security.

Alas, what America really needs is a reverse climate change to good against evil with the strength of determined leadership and limited government. It's a matter of our survival....

VV Daily Press
December 14, 2015

Obama wants to disarm us

President Obama's meaningless babble masks the fact that he wants to disarm Americans more than prevailing against terrorism.

American citizens are arming themselves for defense against criminals and terrorists, and for good reasons. The Obama administration has grossly failed America's domestic and national security by not enforcing border security and the unchecked flow of illegal aliens including criminals and drugs – and conducting an unjust war against our police, diminishing our domestic security.

Indeed, President Obama's feckless foreign policy, apologizing and criticizing America, weakening our military, and exacerbating Islamic terrorism causing the proliferation of ISIS and threats from Iran is increasing the clear and present danger to our homeland, the West and the World. Surely, what needs to end is the era of President Obama's damage to our security, society, our economy and our future.

And that ideology and philosophy of promoting the climate change hustle and disarming Americans must end with the end of Mr. Obama's second term in office.... Meanwhile Americans must be able to exercise their rights to self-defense against all enemies, foreign and domestic. Clearly, in 2016, voters must elect a president who will be a patriot commander in chief. Not a hapless damager in chief.

VV Daily Press
December 4, 2015

Tax and regulation nation

California Governor Brown and President Obama are the amoral poster governor and president for putting our already over-taxed and over-regulated state and nation into overdrive during their corrosive terms in office. Indeed, coupled with an un-American Socialist-Democrat-controlled Legislature and Congress, they have caused overwhelming damage to businesses, the economy and the American people.

Worse, Brown and Obama have recklessly diminished our domestic and national security, with open borders, sanctuary cities, reduced military, and wars against the police. And both continue promoting the climate change hustle, by taxing the economy and our lives. Even worse, while President is responsible for the proliferation of ISIS and terrorism, he blames it on climate change and travels the world criticizing America for everything.

Clearly, our only solution rests with voters, who until now have been dominated by indoctrinated liberals -- who carelessly rubber-stamp the personal power of the enemy within -- blindly committing social, political, moral and economic suicide, taking the rest of us with them. Hopefully, enough damage will wake them up to defending themselves, surviving, recovering and prospering by changing and reducing government to no more than we need.

It is now a matter of life and death....

VV Daily Press
December 1, 2015

County's refugee awareness

Slam the door to terrorists and criminals in California
President Obama urging America to open its arms to Syrian refugees and "….lift them up" is a profound hypocrisy after letting Syrians down in the Syrian civil war creating ISIS and the devastation that followed including the terrorist attacks in Paris. Indeed, California leads the states in Backing the president's efforts.

Therefore, Governor Brown welcoming the most Syrian refugees of any state since the civil war broke out in 2011 comes as no surprise. Furthermore, California has the open door policy to refugees and illegal immigrants, inviting whatever evils that come along with them, from criminals to gangs, to drug smuggling, to human trafficking, and terrorists.

Worse, regardless of the Syrian refugee connection to the Paris terrorist attacks -- and most state governors refusing to accept Syrian refugees -- Governor Brown vowed to work with President Obama in accepting them, leaving our San Bernardino County unaware of most refugees who enter the County.

Even worse, like the illegal alien criminal who murdered a Californian U.S. citizen in San Francisco, with little or no protest from Californians, one wonders how far the controlling Democrat liberal infection here will affect the prevention of ISIS attacks in California, including San Bernardino County and our high desert communities….

It's past time to slam the door to terrorists and criminals in California and America….

VV Daily Press
November 24, 2015

Syrian refugees

Terrorist treachery in Paris. Ten thousand Syrian refugees here?

The tragedy of ISIS terrorist attacks in Paris highlights the alarming advances of fanatical Islamic treachery in the West, furthering their march toward an unencumbered virtual reality of convert or die world domination against infidels.

Worse, the infectious spread of ISIS Sunni's in the Middle East, coupled with competing terrorism from Iranian and Syrian Shiites, backed by Russia, foments historical tribal struggles which can easily metastasize into a coordinated effort against the great Satan – America!

Exacerbated by President Obama's incompetent foreign policy, America's historic role of power in keeping world peace has been compromised by weakness in the Obama administration's, preoccupation with personal power and the blind pursuit of a legacy....

All of which, coupled with Mr. Obama's abdication of responsibility, undermining our energy resources, lack of cyber security, Edward Snowden's treason -- reduced military defense, national security, domestic security – and 7 years of open borders, leaves our country openly vulnerable to terrorism.

Indeed, the inescapable conclusion: Exacerbated by President Obama recklessly accepting 10,000 refugees here -- terrorist included -- adds to ISIS already being here, everywhere and ready to roll....

VV Daily Press
November 17, 2015

America in peril

President Obama made it painfully clear when he helped remove the dictators of Egypt and Libya and encouraged the Arab Spring to spread throughout the Middle East, that he would do nothing about the proliferation of terrorism when he neglected to stop the spread of ISIS from Syria into Iraq.

Furthermore, Mr. Obama endorsed Morsi as president of Egypt, and with it, the Muslim Brotherhood, which resulted in the expansion of al-Qaeda and the entry of ISIS into Egypt -- and most probably, resulted in the bombing of the Russian airliner.

Surely, President Obama is simply not dealing with the aggression and threats from ISIS, Iran or Russia, which creates more and more danger for the world. Most certainly, his unabated incompetence has failed our national and domestic security, which places America in grave, ever-increasing peril.

Alas, the president's feckless administration is in the last round of a legacy that has done serious damage by reducing America to a quasi-socialist state pushing a superficial society of selfish interests, social aggression, political chaos, and economic instability – a perfect handover to a Saul Alinsky-loving first woman president by the name of Hillary Clinton.

That is, if American voters, let it happen....

San Diego Union Tribune
November 16, 2015

Terrorist treachery in Paris -- Ten thousand Syrian refugees here?

The tragedy of ISIS terrorist attacks in Paris highlights the alarming advances of fanatical Islamic treachery in the West, furthering their march toward an unencumbered virtual reality of convert or die world domination against infidels.

President Obama's incompetent foreign policy, America's historic role of power in keeping world peace has been compromised.

All of which, coupled with Mr. Obama's abdication of responsibility, undermining our energy resources, lack of cyber security, Edward Snowden's treason -- reduced military defense, national security, domestic security – and 7 years of open borders, leaves our country openly vulnerable to terrorism.

Exacerbated by President Obama recklessly accepting ten thousand Syrian refugees here -- terrorist included -- adds to ISIS already being here, everywhere and ready to roll....

(Original Letter)

Terrorist treachery in Paris -- Ten thousand Syrian refugees here?

The tragedy of ISIS terrorist attacks in Paris highlights the alarming advances of fanatical Islamic treachery in the West, furthering their march toward an unencumbered virtual reality of convert or die world domination against infidels.

Worse, the infectious spread of ISIS Sunni's in the Middle East, coupled with competing terrorism from Iranian and Syrian Shiites, backed by Russia, foments historical tribal struggles which can easily metastasize into a coordinated effort against the great Satan – America!

Exacerbated by President Obama's incompetent foreign policy, America's historic role of power in keeping world peace has been compromised by weakness in the Obama administration's, preoccupation with personal power and the blind pursuit of a legacy....

All of which, coupled with Mr. Obama's abdication of responsibility, undermining our energy resources, lack of cyber security, Edward Snowden's treason -- reduced military defense, national security, domestic security – and 7 years of open borders, leaves our country openly vulnerable to terrorism.

Indeed, the inescapable conclusion: Exacerbated by President Obama recklessly accepting ten thousand Syrian refugees here -- terrorist included -- adds to ISIS already being here, everywhere and ready to roll....

Riverside Press Enterprise
November 14, 2015

Border control needed

The debate between GOP presidential contenders Donald Trump and Jeb Bush over deporting 12 million illegal immigrants is a moot point, particularly when the fundamental problem has been the lack of border security since President Reagan granted amnesty to 3 million illegal immigrants with the understanding that there would be border security.

Of course, it has become painfully clear that the border was not secured -- coupled with years of feckless attempts at immigration reform -- resulting in the 12 million or more illegal immigrants in America.

And illegal immigration is growing at an alarming rate. Currently, this is because of President Obama's continued record of little or no border enforcement, unsuccessful deportations, and his attempt to grant amnesty to 5 million illegals.

Ironically, Mr. Trump's suggestion to build a border wall would go a long way to solving the problem, particularly because of the increasing threats to our domestic and national security in this age of crime and terrorism.

After all, it is a significant responsibility of the president to resolve problems -- and President Obama creates problems, yet resolves none, which is also Hillary Clinton's main problem....

VV Daily Press
November 10, 2015

True Americans

Monica Kelley's "English" and "Left-wing radicals" letters drive home the points of what America was meant to be. Indeed, English is the American language, as it was meant to be. And we are a constitutional republic of representative democracy, as it was meant to be.

What America is not, is what a half-century of counter-culture revolution of radicals and extremists have done to undermine our nation's constitutional freedoms -- in the name of freedom -- with insidious, vitriolic movements bent on destroying our society with chaos created by our enemies within.

And that is the big-government-socialist way of political indoctrination against conservatives, family, morals and free markets by dividing and conquering, creating a path to tyranny -- propelled by the liberal education establishment, the malicious media and the malignant entertainment industry.

Fortunately, we the people are now more informed and painfully aware of the consequences of the intentional failures of good intentions.

Instead of settling for a superficial society replete with social and political aggression, selfish interests and extremes, we must hold on to our liberty, and keep a tight grip on our freedom. The shame of good deeds is they are not appreciated for generations.

The tragedy of bad deeds is they are not resisted until it's too late. Therefore, as Monica Kelley writes, "Please think before you act. There is a lot going on in this country, and Americans can fix this." Indeed, fixed by true, moral, family, self-reliant, strong, traditional Americans -- as it was always meant to be....

VV Daily Press
November 3, 2015

Monumental abuse of power

Senator Dianne Feinstein and President Obama have abused their power under the Antiquities Act to create massive national monuments to themselves throughout the United States and California restricting recreation and mining on federal lands. Indeed, the Antiquities Act was passed in 1906 to protect "historic landmarks, historic and prehistoric structures and other objects of historic or scientific interest," including sensitive Native American artifacts.

The need for protecting the Grand Canyon with Arizona's proposed Greater Grand Canyon National Heritage Act under the Antiquities Act notwithstanding, there is a need to pass HR 3668, the California Minerals, Off-Road Recreation and Conservation Act, introduced by our California Representative Paul Cook to preserve our majestic landscape, while addressing the needs off-road vehicle users and the protection of economically vital mineral sites.

President Obama's monumental agenda is rooted in his war against coal energy and oil exploration -- with deceptive distractions such as the San Gabriel National Monument, and the recently established 704,000 acre monument in Nevada – while Senator Feinstein focuses on our Mojave Desert lands as her personal monument. Though I'm not a fan of off-road racing and dangerous thrill-seeking, I support people's use of off-road vehicles to safely explore our deserts and mountains – and I certainly support our economic interests in vital minerals and mining.

Surely, we voters must get our act together to reverse and prevent government abuse of power in land-grabbing and in every other respect.

San Diego Union-Tribune
October 30, 2015

GOP candidates are not treated fairly

As the 2016 presidential debates began, Fox News hosted the first GOP debate, which was fair and balanced. Less so, when the second debate was hosted by CNN, which was slanted by the usual liberal-elitist questioning.

Meanwhile, the first Democrat presidential debate hosted by CNN was little more than fawning over the candidates, concluding with the anointing of Hillary Clinton as the first woman president, just as the liberal media did with Barack Obama as the first black president in 2008.

However, the third GOP debate hosted by NBC's business channel CNBC was anything but subtle bias. Rather than concentrating on their specialty, the economy, panel members were condescending, rude, sometimes hostile to the candidates with personal attacks, which came as no surprise from the left.

VV Daily Press
October 27, 2015

Benghazi, Clinton and politics

Hillary Clintons deceptions covering her failings in the Benghazi terrorist attack will not affect her being anointed by the liberal media as the first woman president, just as they did with Barack Obama as the first black president.

The only thing that could derail her candidacy would be an indictment as a result of the FBI/DOJ investigation into her national security email violations, which is unlikely. President Obama won't allow that to taint his manufactured legacy.

Unfortunately for Mr. Obama, true history will not smile kindly upon an unworthy president with a feckless foreign and domestic policy who put America in great peril.

Unfortunately for the American people, if the corrupt Clintons – who let Osama bin-Laden escape and 9/11 to happen, and caused the 2007/2008 crash -- are elected president -- and the Republicans don't finally get their duty to God and country act together -- it could be the end of our history.

The Washington Times
October 26, 2015

Clinton redux would destroy U.S.

Just as Barack Obama's severe shortcomings did not stop the liberal media from anointing him the first black president even before he was elected, Hillary Rodham Clinton's deceptions to cover her failures in the Benghazi terrorist attack will no effect on that same media crowning her the first woman leader of the United States.

The only thing that could derail Mrs. Clinton's candidacy would be an indictment as a result of the FBI/Department of Justice investigation into her email-server violations, and that is unlikely. President Obama won't allow it to taint his manufactured legacy.

Unfortunately for Mr. Obama, true history will not smile kindly upon an unworthy president with a feckless foreign and domestic policy that put America in great peril.

Unfortunately for the American people, if the corrupt Clintons – who let Osama bin-Laden escape and thus caused September 11, 2001 to happen, and caused the 2007/2008 financial crash -- are elected president (and the Republicans don't finally get their duty-to-God-and country act together) it could be the end of our history.

VV Daily Press
October 26, 2015

Failed Afghanistan policy

Against the advice of his generals, President Obama is cutting U.S. forces in Afghanistan by half, but changed his plans to evacuate, leaving 5,000 troops until 2017. That meager force will do nothing to change the plans of the Taliban and ISIS to take-over the country.

And, of course, it will leave the carnage for the next president to deal with.

Bottom line is, President Obama will have handed over the Middle East, Pakistan and Afghanistan to Iran, Russia, ISIS, al-Qaeda and the Taliban to spread terrorism throughout the World, including America. That will be President Obama's legacy.

Riverside Press Enterprise
October 23, 2015

Obama's half-measures still a failure

Re: "U.S. war role to endure" [Front page, Oct. 16]

Against the advice of his generals, President Obama is cutting U.S. forces in Afghanistan by half, but changed his plans to evacuate, leaving 5,000 troops until 2017. That meager force will do nothing to change the plans of the Taliban and ISIS to take-over the country.

And, of course, it will leave the carnage for the next president to deal with.

Bottom line is, President Obama will have handed over the Middle East, Pakistan and Afghanistan to Iran, Russia, ISIS, al-Qaeda and the

Taliban to spread terrorism throughout the World, including America. That will be President Obama's "commander-in-coward" legacy.

VV Daily Press
October 14, 2015

President Obama's perfect record

In President Obama's press conference October 2, 2015, he made it abundantly clear that he will not oppose Putin's military support of Syria's dictator, which is consistent with Obama's perfect record of standing back from the fight against all Islamic terrorist organizations in the Middle East.

Indeed, President Obama's lack of action and weak foreign policy is responsible for the birth of the so-called "Arab Spring" bringing down the dictators of Egypt, Libya and other nations resulting in the proliferation of the Muslim Brotherhood, al-Qaeda, other terrorist groups and the seed and proliferation of ISIS. All of which results in the sad conclusion that, although dictators are mostly bad, in the Islamic Middle East they have historically prevented the terror that reigns there today.

Alas, it is painfully clear that if the Shah of Iran had not been removed by the Ayatollah Khomeini who established a radical Islamic state -- which is now the chief sponsor of terrorism in the world – sworn to destroy Israel and America, our 9/11 efforts in Afghanistan and Iraq would not be so much in vain, and the Middle East would not have exploded into Islamic terrorism against the World.

Add the proliferation of unchecked China and Russian aggression to our enemies mix, President Obama is maintaining a painfully perfect record of tearing down America, disarming us at home and abroad, dangerously reducing our national and domestic security, and thus our freedoms.

San Bernardino Sun
October 2, 2015

Some Thoughts on Pope Francis' visit to U.S.

After reading newspapers, viewing in the news media and then listening to Pope Francis' address to Congress and the United Nations, it was disturbingly obvious that the Pope has been unduly influenced by President Obama regarding, the distribution of wealth, ObamaCare, Cuba relations, the bad Iran deal and Climate Change – which is a social, political and economic shame.

It was, however, heartening to hear Pope Francis' strong support of life at conception, traditional marriage, family and America.

VV Daily Press
September 30, 2015

Motorcycles and the law

The California Legislature must take immediate action to criminalize the dangerous activity of motorcycle gangsters intimidating law-abiding motorists on our freeways and highways, and the similar insanity by dangerous single motorcyclists lane-splitting at 20 to 50 MPH above the flow of traffic. Indeed, they act with total disregard for their own safety and the safety of automobile drivers and their families.

For example, the single reckless driving motorcycle lane-splitters is a daily danger on the freeways, and the motorcycle gangster groups are all too frequent. Recently, my wife and I traveled to Temecula and stopped at a Chevron station near Old Town. The station pumps were completely tied-up by a gang of motorcyclists, some of whom were done with the pumps, but hung around talking to each other causing us to wait nearly 20 minutes for a pump.

After we left looking for a restaurant, one of the gang bikers stopped traffic on a busy road so his fellow gangsters could ride out of a parking lot. The next day, while traveling to our home on the

LETTERS TO THE EDITOR

I-15, a different gang of bikers were dangerously lane-splitting in a group, and when traffic slowed in the freeway construction areas of the Cajon Pass, they rode past recklessly on the inside shoulder of the freeway.

Surely, these are crimes, not traffic infractions. Again, the Legislature and Governor must criminalize this menace, which must be strictly enforced by the CHP and other law enforcement agencies for all our safety. After all, the menacing motorcyclists don't own exclusive rights to the freeways and highways, the motoring, tax paying public does.

Los Angeles Times
September 29, 2015

Pope Francis and his message cross religious and political lines

After reading newspapers, viewing in the news media and then listening to Pope Francis' address to Congress and the United Nations, it was disturbingly obvious that the Pope has been unduly influenced by President Obama regarding, the distribution of wealth, ObamaCare, Cuba relations, the bad Iran deal and Climate Change – which is a social, political and economic shame.

It was, however, heartening to hear Pope Francis' strong support of life at conception, traditional marriage, family and America.

Riverside Press Enterprise
September 25, 2015

Coddling our enemies

President Obama has made it painfully clear that he has no responsibility for America's national and domestic security as evidenced by coddling the Taliban and ISIS, by Russia's aggression in Europe and Syria and his making a bad deal with Iran.

Surely, Obama and family will bask in secure retirement, while his socialist legacy will ensure the demise of our freedom -- unless there is a voter revolt and a concerted conservative rescue and recovery from the 2016 elections. Fiorina and Rubio anyone?

(Original letter)

President Obama coddling our enemies

President Obama has made it painfully clear that he has no responsibility for America's national and domestic security as evidenced by coddling the Taliban (Bowe Bergdahl prisoner exchange); ISIS (allowing them to flourish and run over the Middle East); Russia's aggression in Europe, Syria and assisting Iran's nuclear ambitions; making a bad deal with Iran than will ensure them obtaining nuclear weapons; China undermining our economy, and illegal alien criminals preying on our citizens with impunity.

Indeed, Mr. Obama has intentionally established himself as our greatest threat by turning his back on America and our enemies to pursue his insidious agenda of fundamentally transforming the United States. Surely, Obama and family will bask in secure retirement, while his socialist legacy will ensure the demise of our freedom -- unless there is a voter revolt and a concerted conservative rescue and recovery from the 2016 elections – Fiorina and Rubio anyone?

VV Daily Press
September 25, 2015

2016 rescue needed

President Obama has made it painfully clear that he has no responsibility for America's national and domestic security as evidenced by coddling the Taliban (Bowe Bergdahl prisoner exchange); ISIS (allowing them to flourish and run over the Middle East); Russia's aggression in Europe, Syria and assisting Iran's nuclear ambitions; making a bad deal with Iran than will ensure them obtaining nuclear weapons;

China undermining our economy, and illegal alien criminals preying on our citizens with impunity.

Indeed, Mr. Obama has intentionally established himself as our greatest threat by turning his back on America and our enemies to pursue his insidious agenda of fundamentally transforming the United States. Surely, Obama and family will bask in secure retirement, while his socialist legacy will ensure the demise of our freedom -- unless there is a voter revolt and a concerted conservative rescue and recovery from the 2016 elections – Fiorina and Rubio anyone?

San Diego Union-Tribune
September 19, 2015

Common Core's federal control of education standards

It is common knowledge and well understood that President Obama's establishment of Common Core education standards is a direct move for federal control of public education similar to nationalizing health care with the un-Affordable Care Act.

Indeed, it is also common knowledge that ObamaCareless is seriously damaging to health care, the economy and the American people.

Worse, Common Core Is the final blow of what began as the miseducation of teachers and students in the liberal-socialist counterculture revolution of the 1960's and the subsequent indoctrination of our students, robbing them of a productive education.

Coupled with President Obama's control of energy, finance and housing, the president's fundamental transformation of America is reaching completion, which is frightening....

VV Daily Press
September 17, 2015

Prosecute Clinton gang

Former president Bill Clinton, AG Janet Reno, HUD director and Andrew Cuomo Intimidated banks and mortgage lenders into giving home loans to unqualified buyers to promote Clinton's unaffordable housing scheme, which was carried out by co-conspirator Fannie Mae chairman and CEO, Franklin Raines, and perpetuated by congressional finance chairmen, Barney Frank and Chris Dodd, until the housing and finance crash of 2008. Indeed, Raines consulted with Senator Obama during his campaign for president, and the collapse was wrongly blamed on President Bush and Wall Street – thus Obama won the election.

President Bush attempted to stop the runaway housing problem, but was stopped by Frank and Dodd, who ended up authoring the Dodd/Frank finance act so President Obama could control the banks. The Entire insidious, deceitful plan was perpetuated throughout the Obama administration, which fueled the Occupy Wall Street movement and the call for the prosecution of Wall Street executives. Now late in Obama's distraction legacy game, his Justice Department is targeting executives for prosecution, when they should be targeting the Clinton gang, and probably Obama before the bigger crash comes.

Surely, it's time for big, liberal government's abuse of power to start losing, and for the American people and taxpayers to start winning....

NewsMax Magazine
September 2015 Issue

No sanctuary for criminals

As a retired law enforcement officer, I am outraged by San Francisco's insidious sanctuary policy that caused the murder of an innocent young woman at the hands of a habitual criminal alien with

7 felony convictions and 5 deportations, who was released by San Francisco authorities after felony drug charges were dropped, refusing to honor an ICE hold placed on him.

Indeed, San Francisco is as guilty as the heinous shooter, and should be held responsible. The murderer should be convicted and sentenced to life without parole, period! San Francisco and the feckless State of California, are in dire need of a complete social, political and economic overhaul…. Alas, the loss of this precious life is sad and unforgiveable.

VV Daily Press
September 9, 2015

Stop punishing smokers

It's bad enough that California smokers have endured decades of regulations, being demonized as social outcasts at the hands of liberal political elites, the media and Hollywood – and subjected to punishing taxes such as Rob Reiner's deceitful Prop. 10, which were used for everything but tobacco-related healthcare.

Indeed, at a time when marijuana is on the verge of being legalized, the evil Democrat empire in Sacramento is planning a $2.00 per pack tax which would greatly expand the tyranny against smokers as the California cash cows for government incompetence and waste.

The problem is, the taxes will punish the poor who are smokers more than anyone – alas, the very people Democrats claim they want to help. Surely, California crashing and burning is on track to do just that, exacerbated by forest fire air pollution attacking everyone's health.

Los Angeles Times
September 8, 2015

Another cigarette tax hike: Haven't California smokers paid enough?

It's bad enough that California smokers have endured decades of regulations, being demonized as social outcasts at the hands of liberal political elites, the media and Hollywood – and subjected to punishing taxes such as Proposition 10 in 1998, which did not fund healthcare.

Indeed, at a time when marijuana is on the verge of being legalized, Democrats are planning a $2-per-pack tax that would expand the tyranny against smokers as well as being a cash cow for government incompetence and waste.

The problem is, the taxes will punish the poor who, are smokers more than others – alas, the very people Democrats claim they want to help. Surely, California is on track to crash and burn, exacerbated by forest fire air pollution attacking everyone's health.

Riverside Press Enterprise
September 2, 2015

The war on law enforcement's latest casualty

The ugly ambush and assassination of Deputy Darren Goforth continues the war against police by murderous gangsters throughout the nation.

It is a result of the counter culture revolution of the 1960's, intensified by riots, perpetuated by gangster rappers led by those like Tupac Shakur inciting the assassination of cops, exacerbated by people like former Attorney General Eric Holder and Al Sharpton.

I know this from 41-years of service in law enforcement and the criminal justice system. I am deeply concerned for my friends, family, community, state and country.

Indeed, since President Obama's election, promising to fundamentally transform America, he has pushed our already damaged nation further down a social, political and economic road to legacy-seeking ruin at hyper-speed.

Sadly, America has been deeply infected by the socialist cancer carried by the far-Left's extremists' tyranny of the minority, and the miseducation of our students by indoctrination.

Together with severely weakening our national security in the face of a growing world of terrorism, and the police -- our first line of defense -- our future looks desperately grim.

Hopefully, the people will wake up, and the silent majority will speak up and work to turn it all around – for our survival – and return to what America really means. God bless Deputy Goforth's family and his memory. We must not let his tragic death and all the others be forgotten.

The Washington Times
August 31, 2015

Obama silent on police murder

The unconscionable ambush assassination of Houston Deputy Darren Goforth this week continues the war against police by murderous gangsters throughout the nation. This war is a result of the counter culture revolution of the 1960's, intensified by riots, and perpetuated by gangster rappers such as Tupac Shakur that incited the execution of cops. It has been exacerbated by President Obama's former Attorney Gen Eric H. Holder Jr. and the Rev. Al Sharpton whose actions against local and state law enforcement failed to condemn the escalating the black-against-black gang murders.

I know this from 41-years of service in law enforcement and the criminal justice system, beginning in 1960. I am deeply concerned for the safety of my friends, family, community, state and country. Indeed, since the 2008 presidential election, prior to which Mr. Obama promised to fundamentally transform America, our president has pushed our already damaged nation further and further down a social, political and economic road to ruin. He seeks a legacy at all costs.

Sadly, America has been deeply infected by the socialist cancer of the far left. The miseducation of our students by indoctrination has robbed our next generation of a real education. The current administration continues to move to severely weaken our national security even as we face the global spread of terrorism. Our future looks desperately grim.

Hopefully, the people will wake up, and the silent majority will find its voice prior to next year's presidential election. It must do so for our survival and in order to return to America to its roots.

Mr. Obama spoke out against the murder late last year of the two New York Police Department officers, but he has yet to condemn Deputy Goforth's assassination. The silence is deafening. God bless Deputy Goforth's family and his memory. We must not let his tragic death and all the others be forgotten.

VV Daily Press
August 25, 2015

Clinton's email espionage

Hillary Clinton will likely escape prosecution for her top secret email espionage simply because the Clinton's have "gotten away with murder" since they burst on the political scene in 1992, winning the presidency by default, handed to them by Ross Perot.

Indeed, as a former law enforcement officer since 1960, and since my retirement in 2006, I have witnessed the rise and decline of our country -- including the Clinton "horror story" and President Obama's abysmal terms in office – causing me to be deeply concerned for my family, my country and the American people.

Clearly, It was bad enough that Bill Clinton's silver tongue conned his way passed a long history of sexually abusing women, to accomplish his goals for fame and power, backed by his greedy, ruthless wife and first lady, Hillary -- at any cost.

Alas, that cost included fraudulent land and stock deals, the lives of Arkansas state troopers, White House troubled ally, Vince Foster, surviving impeachment and removal from office, Pardoning America's foremost tax cheat and traitor, Marc Rich, stealing White House property, being the root cause of the 2008 housing and financial collapse, and working the system for personal gain and absolute power.

Coupled with her profitable illegal deals with foreign powers, incompetent service as secretary of state – costing the lives of four Americans including our ambassador at Benghazi, Libya – and receiving classified emails on her private server (tantamount to treason), Hillary Clinton is not qualified to hold public office, particularly the presidency. Clearly, there will be ample evidence to prosecute her.

San Bernardino Sun
August 20, 2015

Time to turn our government around

Re: "Can California cut gasoline usage in half in 15 years? Probably not" (Aug. 12)

California government punishing the populace

Look what's happening to Californians: The California political elite in Sacramento and elsewhere are leading activists, and indoctrinated voters to punishing businesses and the populace with insane laws, which will surely result in a self-imposed collapse of our economy, our security and our society.

Highlighted by the costly miseducation of our students, strangling our energy resources, electricity, transportation, personal and business income with onerous regulations -- deceitful voter-approved Propositions, including a stupid bullet train – Californians are literally under siege by a destructive ideology.

Alas, taken together, Assembly Bill 32 cap and trade, Proposition 30, extreme taxation and now Senate Bill 350 cutting gas use by 50 percent, coupled with AB 109 and Prop. 47 criminal releases and sanctuary cities, and opening prison and jail gates, releasing criminals to prey on the people in the middle of an unjust war against the police, our first line of defense, is bad government that needs to be replaced by limited government and real democracy....

Indeed, at a time when California's authoritarian government is trying to eliminate voters' constitutional rights to initiative, referendum and recall, it's time to turn government around.

VV Daily Press
August 18, 2015

Dynamic trio

In the first Republican debate for president, Gov. Scott Walker, Carly Fiorina and Dr. Ben Carson confirmed their credentials as a dynamic duo who could and should win the 2016 presidential election. Indeed, with either candidate as the nominee for president, and the other as a vice president running mate, they have the capacity and expertise to turn government and the economy around as should have been done decades ago.

Clearly, Gov. Walker has proven himself as a chief state executive officer with the courage and conviction to get results from taking on the tyranny of government and teacher unions, reducing the size of government, cutting taxes and creating jobs, which got him re-elected twice. He is also the only governor who survived a recall election.

Coupled with Newt Gingrich and Gov. John Kasich as his chiefs of staff, Walker would be an ideal president. And surely, Carly Fiorina proved herself as the CEO of HP, the largest tech company in the world, with a deep knowledge of the overall economy, highly capable as vice president to correct government's role. Indeed, Dr. Ben Carson is sorely needed as the Secretary of HHS to deal with Obamacare and to prepare its repeal.

A strong president and administration is just what our country needs to recover from the serious damage inflicted on America's society, economy, domestic and national security by President Obama and his administration, hopefully, before it's too late.... Walker and Fiorina are the best choices to do that.

Sacramento Bee
August 16, 2015

Stewart's damage is permanent

Anyone who has seen and listened to Jon Stewart before he gained fame and influence from his satirical "Daily Show" would know he is, at the core, an angry, vicious, radical socialist, who used his devious talents for a 16-year run on Comedy Central.

Indeed, his political influence poisoned the minds of his young-voter audiences, which gave him the power to lure powerful people and politicians to his table. Hopefully, he will not use that power to continue his cloaked crusade of liberal tyranny in his retirement.

But don't count on it. The infection is permanent, [just as it is with Bill Maher, including their mutual war against religion.]

VV Daily Press
August 15, 2015

Obama's power abuse plan

As promised by President Obama in his 2008 presidential campaign -- stating that he would eliminate coal-power and establish renewable energy, which would necessarily cause people's electricity rates to skyrocket -- Mr. Obama is marching non-stop down the road to fulfilling his legacy at any cost, waving the flag of the global-warming hoax, while he continues fundamentally transforming America, as promised.....

Certainly, coupled with nationalizing health care, over-regulating Wall Street and the finance industry, establishing national education -- and lawlessly circumventing the Constitution and Congress with continuous executive orders and imperial edicts – President Obama's abuse of power seems limitless.

Worse, the president's feckless foreign policy has allowed Russia's aggression to escalate, the al-Qaeda – ISIS terror machines to spread throughout the Middle East and the world, and Iran's state-sponsored terrorism to reign toward nuclear weapons, the destruction of Israel and attacks against America and the West.

Sadly, along with the lack of border security, the infiltration of criminal illegal aliens, socialist chaos, damaging race relations and his war against the police, President Obama Is in the process of pounding the final nails of his legacy into America's social, political, economic, domestic and national security coffin.

Alas, hope is not lost if American voters rise up, reject the liberal disease infecting our country, and take back government in the 2016 elections....

San Diego Union-Tribune
August 14, 2015

Obama's climate plan

Clearly, as promised by President Obama in his 2008 presidential campaign -- stating that he would eliminate coal-power and establish renewable energy, which would necessarily cause people's electricity rates to skyrocket -- Mr. Obama is marching non-stop down the road to fulfilling his legacy, waving the flag of the global-warming hoax as he continues fundamentally transforming America – as promised.

VV Daily Press
August 11, 2015

Trump support retraction

As reader Philip Gericke rightly pointed out, how anyone could be drawn to Donald Trump is difficult to fathom, I am embarrassed and apologize with an explanation: Before the Daily Press published my letter supporting Trump, I submitted a commentary two weeks earlier (July 20) modifying my support to Gov. Scott Walker for president and Carly Fiorina for vice president, a dynamic duo.

Indeed, after watching the first Republic debate, and first question to the candidates, I realized that I was being hustled by Trump, as I painfully recalled being hustled and betrayed by Ross Perot, which had caused me to change from Republican to Independent to support him.

The first Republican debate hosted by Fox News was a great success, revealing the core principles of each candidate, most of whom were highly qualified, with two standouts. First was Carly Fiorina who clearly won the second-tier debate, which should elevate her into the first tier.

Second, and more importantly, was Donald Trump, who disturbingly refused to take the pledge not to run as an independent candidate, which would clearly hand the general election to presumed Democrat nominee, Hillary Clinton, just as Ross Perot did for Bill Clinton to spite George H.W. Bush in 1992.

For that reason, Donald Trump should be scorned and ignored by Republican and most independent voters.

Indeed, the best choices for a Republican presidency should be as follows: Scott Walker, president; Carly Fiorina, Vice President, with major Cabinet positions comprised of: Marco Rubio, Secretary of State; Ted Cruz, Secretary of Defense; Rick Perry, Homeland Security; Chris Christie, Attorney General; John Kasich, Secretary of the Treasury; Ben Carson, Secretary of Health and Human Services; Rand Paul, Secretary of Commerce; and the Department of Education eliminated.

Finally, as a result of the 2016 elections, if Republican don't control the Presidency and the Congress, flaming liberals lit and fueled by President Obama and Hillary Clinton, exacerbated by Russia, China and terrorists, will surely burn down America.

The Washington Times
August 9, 2015

By killing coal, Obama puts final nails in U.S. coffin

As promised in his 2008 presidential campaign, President Obama is marching non-stop down the road to eliminate coal-power and prop up renewable energy, waving the flag of global warming hoax as he goes. This necessarily causes people's electricity rates to sky-rocket. But hey, Mr. Obama is fulfilling his legacy.

Together with nationalizing health care, over-regulating Wall Street and the finance industry, establishing national education and circumventing the Constitution and Congress with continuous exec-utive orders and imperial edicts, Mr. Obama's abuse of power seems limitless.

Worse, the president's feckless foreign policy has allowed Russia's aggression to escalate, the al-Qaeda- Islamic-State- terror machines to spread throughout the Middle East and elsewhere the world, and Iran's state-sponsored terrorism to move more feasibly toward nuclear weapons, the destruction of Israel and attacks against America and the West.

Alas, along with the lack of border security, the infiltration of crim-inal illegal aliens, socialist chaos, and his war against the police, Mr. Obama Is in the process of pounding the final nails of his legacy into America's social, political, economic, domestic and national security coffin.

USA TODAY
August 7, 2015

Re: Climate change: Obama plan worth the cost?

As President Obama promised in his first presidential campaign, he is marching non-stop down the road to fulfilling his legacy at any cost, waving the flag of global-warming alarmism, while he continues fundamentally transforming America. Certainly, coupled with nation-alizing health care and over-regulating Wall Street and the finance industry President Obama's abuse of power seems limitless.

Worse, the president's feckless foreign policy has allowed Russia's aggression to escalate, terror machines to spread throughout the Middle East and the world, and Iran's state-sponsored terrorism to move toward nuclear weapons, the destruction of Israel and attacks against America and the West.

Hope is not lost if American voters rise up, reject the liberal views infecting our country, and take back government in the next election.

Riverside Press Enterprise
August 6, 2015

Obama's abuse of power

Re: " A fact-challenged clean energy plan" [Editorial, Aug. 8]: As promised by President Obama in his 2008 presidential campaign -- stating that he would eliminate coal-power and establish renewable energy, which would necessarily cause people's electricity rates to skyrocket -- Mr. Obama is marching non-stop down the road to fulfilling his legacy at any cost, waving the flag of the global-warming hoax, while he continues fundamentally transforming America, as promised.

Certainly, coupled with nationalizing health care, over-regulating Wall Street and the finance industry, establishing national education -- and lawlessly circumventing the Constitution and Congress with continuous executive orders and imperial edicts – President Obama's abuse of power seems limitless.

Worse, the president's feckless foreign policy has allowed Russia's aggression to escalate, the al-Qaeda – ISIS terror machines to spread throughout the Middle East and the world, and Iran's state-sponsored terrorism to reign toward nuclear weapons, the destruction of Israel and attacks against America and the West.

Sadly, along with the lack of border security, the infiltration of criminal illegal aliens, socialist chaos, damaging race relations and his war against the police, President Obama Is in the process of pounding the final nails of his legacy into America's social, political, economic, domestic and national security coffin.

Alas, hope is not lost if American voters rise up, reject the liberal disease infecting our country, and take back government in the 2016 elections....

VV Daily Press
August 3, 2015

Trump's truth for president

The demonization of Donald Trump by America's insidious Left comes as no surprise, particularly, when Trump hits that liberal nerve. Indeed, the attacks are increasing and relentless, even to blatantly violating his constitutional conservative free speech and property rights.

Does that bother Mr. Trump? Absolutely not. Since announcing his candidacy for president, he has aggressively taken on all comers from the liberal media, to divisive racial agitators, business cowards, and spineless Republicans.

Clearly, what America and the Republican Party need to recover from President Obama's terrible-terms in office, damaging Democrats and the anti-American Left is "The Donald" playing his patriotic Trump cards against all enemies, foreign and domestic.

Surely, with a solid VP such as Sen. Rubio or Gov. Walker, a president Trump would take-on economy-busting big government, build strong national security and restore the economy. Certainly, the TRUTH is what America needs to triumph over evil. And Trump's got it!

VV Daily Press
July 24, 2015

Governor's sky is falling

In a blind pursuit of his "sky is falling" legacy, Governor Brown has assumed the role of the leader of environmental zealot movement by increasing the negative economic impact of AB-32's carbon tax. However, that wasn't enough. The governor is now riding the moonbeam of SB-350 legislation that will impose even more abuse of power by requiring half of the state's electricity be generated from costly, unreliable renewable resources by 2030.

Indeed, with Governor Brown's climate change goals, it doesn't matter that there will be an enormous impact on the economy and cost of living. No, there's more to SB-350, which requires a 50 percent cut in the consumption of gasoline, to be administered by the governor's appointed, California Air Resources Board. Worse, there is nothing in SB-350 to prevent gasoline rationing.

Alas, it's bad enough that California already has the highest gasoline prices and gas tax in the by 1 dollar per gallon over the national average. And that California will not allow the construction of new oil refineries, or adding new oil and natural gas resources. Or that California's Green additive blend of gasoline is not only costly, but damaging to vehicle engines. Now, Mr. Brown's hit team wants to stick oil companies with an oil extraction tax.

Clearly, the sky's the limit for Californian's cost of living.

San Bernardino Sun
July 24, 2015

Gov. Brown's ambitious climate change goals

Re: "Climate change battle to get harder" (July 19)

In a blind pursuit of his "sky is falling" legacy, Governor Brown has assumed the role of the leader of environmental zealot movement by increasing the negative economic impact of Assembly Bill 2's carbon tax.

However, that wasn't enough. The governor is now riding the moonbeam of Senate Bill 350 legislation that will impose even more abuse of power by requiring half of the state's electricity be generated from costly, unreliable renewable resources by 2030.

Indeed, with Gov. Brown's climate change goals, it doesn't matter that there will be an enormous impact on the economy and cost of living. No, there's more to SB 350, which requires a 50 percent cut in the consumption of gasoline, to be administered by the governor's appointed, California Air Resources Board. Worse, there is nothing in SB-350 to prevent gasoline rationing.

It's bad enough that California already has the highest gasoline prices and gas tax in the by 1 dollar per gallon over the national average. And that California will not allow the construction of new oil refineries, or adding new oil and natural gas resources. Or that California's green additive blend of gasoline is not only costly, but damaging to vehicle engines. Now, Mr. Brown's hit team wants to stick oil companies with an oil extraction tax.

Clearly, the sky's the limit for Californian's cost of living.

VV Daily Press
July 21, 2015

Terror in Tennessee

The terrorist attack in Tennessee is making it painfully clear that President Obama's ambivalence to the deadly reality of the immediate and growing danger to America from Islamic terrorists -- including the threat from within -- is putting our nation in peril and endangering our people. Indeed, treating terrorist attacks such as Fort Hood, the Boston Marathon, Texas and others as work place violence and crimes rather than blatant terrorism is a serious dereliction of duty.

Coupled the Obama administration's direct complicity in the lack of border security, the fall of the Middle East to terrorists, capitulating to Iran's pursuit of nuclear weapons -- our failing national defense and security -- and pursuing his ideological "Internet Neutrality" to limit conservative speech instead of having his FCC, FBI, CIA and Homeland Security vigorously defend against terrorism, Russia and China's cyber-attacks against us -- is indefensible and un-American.

Alas, Hillary Clinton would do no better – probably worse, considering her complicity in failed foreign policy.

Riverside Press Enterprise
July 18, 2015

America cannot ignore threat of Islamic terrorism

Re: "Four Marines slain, may be an act of terror" [Front page, July 17}. The terrorist attack in Tennessee is making it painfully clear that President Obama's ambivalence to the deadly reality of the immediate and growing danger to America from Islamic terrorists -- including the threat from within -- is putting our nation in peril and endangering our people.

Indeed, treating terrorist attacks such as Fort Hood, the Boston Marathon, Garland, Texas and others as work place violence and crimes rather than blatant terrorism is a serious dereliction of duty.

Coupled the Obama administration's direct complicity in the lack of border security, the fall of the Middle East to terrorists, capitulating to Iran's pursuit of nuclear weapons, our failing national defense and security and pursuing his ideological Internet neutrality instead of having the government vigorously defend against terrorism and Russia and China's cyber-attacks against us.

It is indefensible and un-American.

Alas, Hillary Clinton would do no better – probably worse, considering her complicity in failed foreign policy.

VV Daily Press
July 17, 2015

City kills innocent woman

As a retired law enforcement officer, I am outraged by San Francisco's insidious sanctuary policy that caused the murder of an innocent young woman at the hands of a habitual criminal alien with 7 felony convictions and 5 deportations, who was released by San Francisco authorities after felony drug charges were dropped, refusing to honor an ICE hold placed on him.

It's bad enough that California's open door to illegal aliens is costing taxpaying citizens $billions to provide education, healthcare, housing and welfare – much more in terms of crime and drugs – exacerbated by President Obama's open border failure to protect our citizens from the predators. Legal pursuit of citizenship notwithstanding, it's time to slam the door on the invasion.

Indeed, San Francisco is as guilty as the heinous shooter, and should be held responsible. The murderer should be convicted and sentenced to death. Even though he won't be executed, at least he will serve life without parole, which is redundant as is San Francisco and the feckless State of California, in dire need of a complete social, political and economic overhaul....

Alas, the loss of this precious life is sad and unforgiveable.

Riverside Press Enterprise
July 13, 2015

Greece betrayed Democracy

Since the birth of Democracy in 5th Century BC, Athens by Pericles, Greece has betrayed democracy by using it to establish a self-destructive society strangled by self-imposed socialism. Indeed, the Greek people became too reliant on government providing them with all the benefits of living without responsibility, and rejecting government austerity.

Clearly, in the centuries since the success of Pericles direct democracy, it has been demonized as being the tyranny of the majority and the people voting themselves largess. However, a socialist-style society is vulnerable to be consumed by Communism, wherein a dictatorship government owns everything, including the people, who have no rights, no property, and become slaves of the state.

Alas, the world knows that through many years of tyrannical monarchies, the dictatorial socialism/fascism such as Germany and Italy -- and the scourge of Communist Russia, China, North Korea and Cuba -- are the mortal enemies of freedom.

Indeed, America became the hope of the world by separating from a monarchy with a revolutionary war and establishing a unique constitutional republic of representative democracy and all the freedoms that came with it -- for as long as we could hold on to it. And we have, against and all enemies, foreign and domestic. Yet, even here, the tyranny of the minority and the evils of socialism have grown and persist with indoctrination, government growth and the abuse of power.

Surely, with the additional threat of terrorism against us, we have reached critical crossroads and must recover and survive. The only way to do that is to truthfully inform the people and establish a direct representative democracy, wherein professional government managers – not politicians – are elected. They must be confirmed each year, and must truthfully inform the voters. Voters would decide all matters of taxation and public policy. We can do that with a 28th Amendment to the Constitution.

Greece lost its roots of democracy and failed. America cannot to the same.

VV Daily Press
July 10, 2015

Obama's monarchial legacy

President Obama is making it painfully clear that he will leave a monarchial legacy of social, political and economic pain, severely diminished national and domestic security -- and racial divisions. Indeed, of elected, Hillary Clinton would leave a similar legacy including gender divisions.

A Republican president and Congress would reverse Mr. Obama's executive abuse of power, recover the economy, national and domestic security, simplify the tax code, reduce spending and the national debt, limit government, rescue education and ameliorate racial discontent.

The dangerous alternative is for the electorate to commit voter-assisted social, political and economic suicide.

VV Daily Press
July 2, 2015

Forest Service is no service

The Lake Fire near Big Bear Lake, which started before 4PM, June 17, 2015, blew up overnight and quickly grew from 500 acres to 10,000 acres was exacerbated by Forest Service refusal to control Bark Beetles, the neglect to have immediate access to Super Scooper and DC 10 water tankers, and the overall incompetence of Forest Service fire-fighting and control burns gone out of control. The fire has since surpassed 30,000 acres and still burning.

Indeed, every major fire in Southern California – including the Rim Fire, Old Fire, Station Fire, Oak Hills fire, San Diego and Orange County fires -- would not have raged out-of-control if they had of been extinguished immediately by massive fire retardant and water drops. And they would not have burned so quickly, if it were not for dead trees killed by Bark Beetles, and the Forest Service's refusal to thin forests.

Cal Fire, county and city fire departments notwithstanding, there is simply no excuse for the Forest Service not to own and distribute sufficient water dropping DC 10's and Super Scoopers, rather than skimping on leasing them, and failing to activate them immediately to forest fires. Clearly, the Forest Service's overall incompetence and irresponsibility are why the Lake Fire and other major fires raged and exploded.

Coupled with the loss of life, property and damage to people's health, the Forest Service is no service in fire prevention and forest fires -- is costly, outrageous and unacceptable -- not so different from all big government. Alas, as a retired law enforcement officer and former fire dispatcher, I can say that the environmentalist-friendly news media's silence on these critical matters is destructively deafening....

The Washington Times
June 29, 2015

In 2016, one way out

President Obama is making it painfully clear that he will leave a monarchial legacy of social, political and economic pain, severely diminished national and domestic security -- and racial divisions. Indeed, of elected, Hillary Clinton would leave a similar legacy including gender divisions.

A Republican president and Congress would reverse Mr. Obama's executive abuse of power, recover the economy, national and domestic security, simplify the tax code, reduce spending and the national debt, limit government, rescue education and ameliorate racial discontent.

The dangerous alternative is for the electorate to commit voter-assisted social, political and economic suicide.

San Diego Union-Tribune
June 27, 2015

President Obama's monarchial legacy

President Obama is making it painfully clear that he will leave a monarchial legacy of social, political and economic pain, severely diminished national and domestic security -- and racial divisions. Indeed, of elected, Hillary Clinton would leave a similar legacy including gender divisions.

A Republican president and Congress would reverse Mr. Obama's executive abuse of power, recover the economy, national and domestic security, simplify the tax code, reduce spending and the national debt, limit government, rescue education and ameliorate racial discontent.

The dangerous alternative is for the electorate to commit voter-assisted social, political and economic suicide.

San Diego Union-Tribune
June 26, 2015

Supreme Court betrays America again

Chief Justice Roberts -- nominated by President Bush – was a stealth liberal in conservative clothing as evidenced by upholding nationalized Obamacare twice along with other rulings in conflict with the law and the Constitution.

Worse, Chief Justice Roberts' deeply-flawed reasoning for the decision was based upon the people electing a Congress to enact Obamacare, even though it was done by a Democrat majority behind closed doors with no debate.

Indeed, the liberal super-majority on the Court is blatantly supporting President Obama's monarchial mandate to fundamentally transform America from a constitutional republic into a socialist nation.

Surely, Roberts' Court will back President Obama's legacy as the first black president, regardless of the social, political, economic and constitutional harm to America and the people.

VV Daily Press
June 19, 2015

Obama's policy conflicts

President Obama has made it abundantly clear that his foreign policy is no policy -- but taking a dangerous path to eliminating American power and influence in a world of aggressive nations and Jihadist terrorism – diminishing our military defenses and sacrificing our national security.

In stark contrast, President Obama has made it painfully clear that his domestic policy is replete with the abuse of executive authority, orders and edicts, regardless of constitutional limitations, the law and the consequences.

Indeed, his latest EPA edict is to seize control of millions of acres of private land water rights. Coupled with his costly war against global warming and the police, our domestic security in serious peril.

Riverside Press Enterprise
June 16, 2015

Protect data instead of policing Internet

When President Obama's FCC chairman says there will now be a "Net Neutrality" referee to keep the Internet fast, fair and open, what he really means is that it will be highly regulated as a telecommunications utility that will soon be taxed like telephone service.

Worse, the referee will in fact become a socialist government bully with a biased agenda to control Internet content and inhibit free speech -- particularly conservative speech, while allowing ISIS recruiting to run wild.

What government should be doing, is concentrating on protecting secrets, records and the people against criminal hackers and terrorists with the very best step-ahead security, and punishing violators, instead of business-as-usual government incompetence.

Losing all government personnel and selective defense records to Chinese and Russian espionage is unconscionable. Indeed, Hillary-style hiding won't cut it.

Los Angeles Times
June 7, 2015
(Lead letter)

The TSA's usefulness

Re: "Time for the TSA to go?." Opinion, June 5

It is highly disturbing and unacceptable that Transportation Security Administration agents failed to detect 95% of firearms and explosives concealed by operatives in tests.

Worse, the TSA director was reassigned rather than removed from government employment. The solution, of course, is to remove the costly bureaucracy and layers of useless administration impeding Homeland Security and the TSA. Surely, there is no place for bloated, over-reaching incompetency, abuse of authority or dereliction of duty from those responsible for our national security.

In terms of the TSA, it should be replaced by airport security divisions of local law enforcement -- such as the airport police covering Los Angeles airports -- which could be extended to passenger screening and complete security at airports. Our security demands it.

NEWSMAX Magazine
June 2015 issue

Obama regulations

ObamaCare, ObamaFinance, ObamaEnergy, and now the ObamaNet are making it painfully clear that President Obama's ObamAmerica and leftist Democrats – including Hollywood -- are the party of tyranny against the best interests of the American people with destructive regulations, punishing taxation and unsustainable national debt. ("President Obama, You're no Ronald Reagan," March).

(original letter)

ObamaCare, ObamaFinance, ObamaEnergy, and now the ObamaNet are making it painfully clear that President Obama's ObamAmerica and leftist Democrats – including Hollywood -- are the party of tyranny against the best interests of the American people with destructive regulations, punishing taxation and unsustainable national debt.

Worse, President Obama's legacy is on reckless course to disarm the United States in the face of dictator Putin's Russian aggression, a rapidly expanding Islamic terrorist movement – feigned negotiations with Iran's nuclear weapons state, regardless of Israeli President Netanyahu's real warnings – all of which threaten to annihilate Israel, America and the West.

Clearly, it's bad enough that the counter-culture revolutionists have turned our country into a superficial society of social injustice, political chaos, selfish interests, economic instability/uncertainty, and extremes. Indeed, developing a nation of fools by indoctrination, distractions, deceptions, lies, the insidious intended consequences of failed good intentions, and the loss of freedoms is what a socialist takeover is all about.

Alas, the next two years will be our nation's reckoning with the enemy within the 7th round of President Obama and his minions vs. America, with only the Republican Party and the informed people standing in the way of an 8th round knockout. Attention: Republican Congress, governors and presidential nominee! Strong language and action is what is needed -- for our survival and restoration. The washed-out Washington way simply won't cut it!

VV Daily Press
June 1, 2015

Foreign policy is no policy

To say that ISIS running wild in the Middle East with impunity, and that Russia, China and Iran's aggression have dramatically increased is the unintended consequences of President Obama's lack of leadership in the world is a generous conclusion.

President Obama's ideological agenda to eliminate American leadership, power and influence in the world is intended, regardless of the consequences, including the threats to our national security.

In Addition, the clear and present consequences for President Obama's over-reaching regulations and executive actions regarding health care, illegal immigration, climate change, limiting free enterprise and the war against police are seriously damaging our freedoms, our economy and our domestic security.

Indeed, President Obama's foreign policy is no policy. And his domestic policy is tantamount to tyranny. God bless and save America. President Obama can't. Alas, he won't.

VV Daily Press
May 29, 2015

Highway robbery

It has become painfully clear that government's freeway projects on Interstate 15, the 215 and other highways are the products of misfeasance, particularly from the Cajon Pass, South through San Bernardino and Riverside Counties.

Indeed, other than the 215 bottlenecks in San Bernardino, the mostly unnecessary road construction on the 15 and 215 have exacerbated impeding traffic, endangering motorists with narrow lanes and confusing interchanges, a total lack of consideration, unreasonably time-consuming projects and the enormous cost to taxpayers – at least ten times over.

Surely, the conclusion can only be that, other than maintenance and repairs, there was no reason for the massive projects. Clearly, the years of highway robbery must be stopped. Taxpaying voters can be the new sheriff in town to get it done.

Riverside Press Enterprise
May 26, 2015

State awash in taxes and overregulation

Our country is wrought with over-reaching taxes and regulations. As usual, California is first in the nation in leading the assault against once-free enterprise and the middle class by government and environmental extremists

It wasn't enough for Governor Brown to destroy Gov. Ronald Reagan's pro-business and middle class economy, and the best public education in the nation.

In his first term. Brown permanently set back public education by authorizing teachers to unionize.

Proposition 98 sealed funding obligations, and the insidious conflict of interest political contributions to Brown and other Democrats followed, resulting in the worst and most costly public education system in the country.

Adding costly insult to injury, Proposition 30's taxation and Assembly Bill 32's carbon tax, cap and trade extortion -- using the global warming hoax -- are aimed at filling big government coffers with the tax and spending fraud, exacerbating energy costs, the drought, the cost to small business, and the cost of living.

Certainly, the failures and government aggression of Gov. Brown, the Democrat Legislature -- President Obama's health-care-less act, the onerous Dodd-Frank finance act, reckless foreign policy and national defense failures -- and overall assaults against our economy are overwhelming evidence of the clear and present danger to our domestic and national security.

Alas, naïve and indoctrinated voters must wake up, wise up and make changes happen or we all suffer the consequences.

So, it's either freedom lost, or work and vote for recovery, liberty, prosperity and justice for all.

Riverside Press Enterprise
May 25, 2015

Stephanopoulos and Clinton

George Stephanopoulos and James Carville were the lead team for Bill Clinton's 1992 presidential campaign. Remember the campaign slogan, "It's the economy, stupid!" George was Clinton's communications director and stepped down after Clinton's 1996 re-election.

As for Bill and Hillary's current bid for the presidency, why is there no news coverage about Bill Clinton's presidency causing the 2008 housing and financial crash?

Former president Clinton and his Janet Reno/Andrew Cuomo hit squad intimidated banks, mortgage lenders and Fannie Mae into making home loans to unqualified buyers in their reckless drive for affordable housing.

Obviously, it was unaffordable housing. And our nation is still paying for it.

San Diego Union-Tribune
May 24, 2015

Autonomy proposal borders on ridiculous

Beware! San Diego activist, Louis J. Marinelli has received approval to gather signatures for his initiative, "A new hope for California," which would make our state an autonomous region like Scotland is to the United Kingdom.

However, Mr. Marinelli is apparently lost in the liberal wilderness, or he would realize that California is already an autonomous nation-state.

Indeed, his voter-initiative would probably pass with a naïve freedom-crushing liberal majority, ratifying our authoritarian state ruled by President Jerry Brown, his socialist Legislature and the economy-crushing environmentalists.

Clearly, what the suicidal "California crashing" people fail to recognize is that their Democrat-voter-seeking open border is rapidly evolving into a nation-state of Mexico.

Alas, it's time for Californians to wise-up before it's too late.

Riverside Press Enterprise
May 22, 2015

Extremism exacerbates state's drought

California's extended drought is meaningless to extreme environmentalist-driven government regulations, which has cost a single sea water desalination plant in Carlsbad near San Diego a 10-year delay in completing the plant because of 6-years of frivolous environmental lawsuits. Indeed, insidious lawsuits and onerous government regulations have prevented the plant from producing 54 million gallons of water per day.

Poseidon Water's Carlsbad desalination plant is the largest in North America and is slated to go online this Fall. Obviously, California government and environmental terrorists have been recklessly irresponsible by further exacerbating California's extended drought by allowing millions of acre feet of water to flow into the ocean to protect a tiny fish, ignoring other water resources, our extended coastline and the worldwide use of desalination.

Clearly, there must be a reversal of decades of environmentalist voter-assisted economic suicide. It's time to turn back to the prosperity of California's gold instead of blindly pursuing a fool's paradise – a terminal liberal affliction.

VV Daily Press
May 20, 2015

Regulation roadblock

California's extended drought is meaningless to extreme environmentalist-driven government regulations, which has cost a single sea water desalination plant in Carlsbad near San Diego a 10-year delay in completing the plant because of 6-years of frivolous environmental lawsuits. Indeed, insidious lawsuits and onerous government regulations have prevented the plant from producing 54 million gallons of water per day.

Poseidon Water's Carlsbad desalination plant is the largest in North America and is slated to go online this Fall. Obviously, California government and environmental terrorists have been recklessly irresponsible by further exacerbating California's extended drought by allowing millions of acre feet of water to flow into the ocean to protect a tiny fish, ignoring other water resources, our extended coastline and the worldwide use of desalination.

Surely, Californians should take notice of Israel's success in resolving their water shortages in 5 years by providing half their water supply with desalination plants producing 100 billion gallons of water per year. Clearly, there must be a reversal of decades of environmentalist voter-assisted economic suicide. It's time to turn back to the prosperity of California's gold instead of blindly pursuing a fool's paradise – a terminal liberal affliction.

Los Angeles Times
Opinion L.A.
May 18, 2015

California's regulation roadblock to water and prosperity

California's extended drought is meaningless to extreme environmentalist-driven government regulations, which has cost a single sea water desalination plant in Carlsbad near San Diego a 10-year delay in completing the plant because of 6-years of frivolous environmental lawsuits. Indeed, insidious lawsuits and onerous government regulations have prevented the plant from producing 54 million gallons of water per day.

Poseidon Water's Carlsbad desalination plant is the largest in North America and is slated to go online this Fall. Obviously, California government and environmental terrorists have been recklessly irresponsible by further exacerbating California's extended drought by allowing millions of acre feet of water to flow into the ocean to protect a tiny fish, ignoring other water resources, our extended coastline and the worldwide use of desalination.

Surely, Californians should take notice of Israel's success in resolving their water shortages in 5 years by providing half their water supply with desalination plants producing 100 billion gallons of water per year. Clearly, there must be a reversal of decades of environmentalist voter-assisted economic suicide. It's time to turn back to the prosperity of California's gold instead of blindly pursuing a fool's paradise – a terminal liberal affliction.

VV Daily Press
May 17, 2015

Bravo for stance

USA TODAY's May 6th editorial concluding that, "At a moment in history when terrorism is close to inevitable, the lesson from Texas is that only fools invite it while wiser men prepare," is a vital lesson that should be heeded by the ideological fools who provoked the terrorist attack in Garland, Texas, and everywhere.

Indeed, rather than being prepared, President Obama's foolish foreign policy and intentional national security and defense weakness has invited and provoked the rapid growth and spread of terrorism throughout the world. And surely, his lack of support of our police is deeply troubling.

Thankfully, the editorial went on to commend the alert Texas police officer who killed the two terrorists before they reached their target and saved countless lives. Fortunately, suggesting that he should be cloned isn't really necessary because the police are prepared to protect and serve as our first line of defense.

I know this as a retired sheriff's sergeant, detective personnel officer and academy instructor with 41 years of service.

Bravo, USA TODAY. Keep it up and lighten-up on the liberal bent. It's unbecoming for the nation's newspaper.

VV Daily Press
May 14, 2015

Rush to judgment

Re: "Baltimore state's attorney indicts and convicts police for homicide".... It was bad enough that the Baltimore mayor handcuffed the police to give rioters space to loot and destroy, and incited violence against officers in response to the tragic death of Freddie Gray while in custody.

Worse, the young and reckless Baltimore state's attorney has made a rush to judgment by filing homicide charges against the 6 officers involved in the incident, convicting the officers, while boasting to the young rioters that, "This is our time."

Clearly, it is painfully obvious that the Baltimore mayor is a star to the irresponsible element of the black community, and that the state's attorney is a rising superstar, advancing her political ambitions.

Indeed, this rush to injustice is looking more like a lynching of police, while the Baltimore mayor declares that this is a model for the nation to follow. Sadly, President Obama, Al Sharpton and others have directly and indirectly caused the rise in racial unrest and the insidious war against police in America.

San Bernardino Sun
May 14, 2015

Time for California to cash in on Columbia River water

With 86 billion gallons of Columbia River water per day flowing into the ocean, there is certainly a need to divert much of that water to drought-stricken California to meet the needs of Northern Californians, Central Valley farmlands and the people of Southern California.

Clearly, there must be combined cooperation between the Federal Bureau of Water Reclamation serving the Central Valley Water Project, the California State Water Resources Control Board, and the California State Water Project to accomplish what is needed.

Surely, between the Columbia River, Klamath River, Lake Shasta and the Sacramento Delta, a series of pipelines and reservoirs can be constructed to bring, store and deliver all the necessary water to resolve our long term problems.

First, however, Governor Brown and unreasonable environmental extremists must get their act together for the good of the people. Governor Brown should quit over-feeding such things as the miseducation money pit, scrap his $68 billion bullet train, add the $7.3 billion water project funds and begin the real California water project in earnest.

Indeed, California voters should demand it for our survival.

VV Daily Press Dispatch
May 3, 2015

Rioters respond to mayor (unedited)

As a retired law enforcement officer with 41 years of experience in the criminal justice system, including the Watts Riot, I am appalled by Baltimore Mayor Stephanie Rawlings-Blake giving "space" -- license to those demonstrating about the tragic death of Freddie Gray -- "to destroy."

Indeed, Mayor Rawlings-Blake's unconscionable behavior spurred cause to inciting riots, looting businesses, burning 15 buildings and 144 vehicles – including police cars – and seriously injuring 15 police officers with rocks the size of tennis balls. Five officers are still hospitalized.

Further, it was tantamount to the reckless behavior of President Obama's counselor on race-relations, Al Sharpton inciting riots in Ferguson, Missouri, New York Mayor de Blasio doing the same, resulting in the assassinations of two New York police officers, and President Obama himself causing division against the police and being late in condemning the violence of rioters.

Clearly, the rioters in Baltimore throwing rocks were assaults with deadly weapons, which could have lawfully resulted in police firing upon the rock-throwers in self-defense. Alas, my heart goes out to the brave police, our first line of defense, and to the brave, responsible mother who physically disciplined her son for throwing rocks.

Daniel B. Jeffs
Apple Valley

Riverside Press Enterprise
April 30, 2015

Baltimore mayor's role in rioting

As a retired law enforcement officer with 41 years of experience in the criminal justice system, including the Watts Riot, I am appalled by Baltimore Mayor Stephanie Rawlings-Blake giving "space" -- license to those demonstrating about the tragic death of Freddie Gray -- "to destroy."

Indeed, Mayor Rawlings-Blake's unconscionable behavior spurred riots, looting businesses, burning 15 buildings and 144 vehicles – including police cars – and seriously injuring 15 police officers with rocks the size of tennis balls, 5 of whom are still hospitalized.

Further, it was tantamount to the reckless behavior of President Obama's counselor on race-relations, Al Sharpton, inciting riots in Ferguson, Mo, New York Mayor Bill de Blasio doing the same, resulting in the assassinations of two New York police officers, and President Obama himself causing division against the police and being late in condemning the violence of rioters.

Clearly, the rioters in Baltimore throwing rocks were assaults with deadly weapons, which could have lawfully resulted in police defending themselves.

Alas, my heart goes out to the brave police, our first line of defense, and to the brave, responsible mother who physically disciplined her son for being involved in the riot and throwing rocks.

VV Daily Press
April 29, 2015

Limit government (unedited)

Preceded by government growth under Presidents Teddy Roosevelt, the 16th income tax Amendment, Woodrow Wilson, Franklin D. Roosevelt and Lyndon B. Johnson, six years of the Obama administration's government growth, debt, abuse of power, abject domestic and foreign policy failure -- backed by the liberal media and blind allegiance of a Democrat Congress -- have metastasized the tumors of liberal government growth into a terminal case of social, political, economic and national security cancer.

Even though there was a revival under President Reagan, the Newt Gingrich congressional Contract with America, and the American people have since elected another Republican Congress to fight the liberal disease, President Obama has made it painfully clear that he will not be deterred from finishing his legacy terms in office, regardless of the consequences, which are forthcoming social, political, economic and national security disasters.

There is but one cure for these cancers, and that is to significantly reduce and limit the size, scope and power of government over our lives, by electing a president and vice-president, and tougher Republican Congress to take on the extremely difficult jobs of real leadership, undeterred – which will take a full two terms -- with a follow-up presidency and Congress.

Indeed, "It's time for a change" is no longer a hackneyed phrase in these critical times of social, political, economic and moral decay brought on by the counter cultural revolution of the 1960's. We must recover our social compatibility, political integrity, economic growth, military and foreign policy strength with true leadership and simply getting it done.

At this point, in the 2016 presidential elections, those leaders appear to be Gov. Scott Walker, Sen. Marco Rubio and Carly Fiorina. So, my fellow Americans, let's wake up and get it done for our survival and the survival of our nation – and recover the land of the free and home of the brave.

Los Angeles Times
Opinion LA
April 28, 2015

Columbia River pipeline

With 86 billion gallons of Columbia River water per day flow-ing into the ocean, there is certainly a need to divert much of that water to drought-stricken California to meet the needs of Northern Californians, Central Valley farmlands and the people of Southern California.

Clearly, there must be combined cooperation between the Federal Bureau of Water Reclamation serving the Central Valley Water Project, the California State Water Resources Control Board, and the California State Water Project to accomplish what is needed.

Surely, between the Columbia River, Klamath River, Lake Shasta and the Sacramento Delta, a series of pipelines and reservoirs can be constructed to bring, store and deliver all the necessary water to resolve our long term problems.

First, however, Governor Brown and unreasonable environmental extremists must get their act together for the good of the people. Governor Brown should quit over-feeding such things as the mise-ducation money pit, scrap his $68 billion bullet train, add the $7.3 billion water project funds and begin the real California water project in earnest.

Indeed, California voters should demand it for our survival.

VV Daily Press
April 26, 2015

The threat from within

It is frightening to realize that the counter-culture, anti-establish-ment boomers of the 1960's and 70's have become an undermining threat to the survival of America from the shroud of the miseducation establishment, the tyranny of anti-Capitalism socialists, and the insidious growth of government.

Worse, the counter-cultural revolution has turned America into a superficial society of government dependency, social aggression, political hostility, relentlessly assaulted by selfish interests and the failures of good intentions.

It should be noted that Bill and Hillary Clinton are from the first of the Boomer generation, and President Obama is from the last of the generation. Enough said.

Indeed, our nation is steeped in uncertainty, and our freedom is fleeting from a deadly second front -- which is being fatally demonstrated by the new barbarians on the block -- who are the world-domination Jihadists of radical Islam obsessed with eliminating non-believers from the face of the earth at any cost.

Alas, it has been said, and how true it is, that the only thing necessary for evil to triumph is for good people to remain silent and do nothing.

Therefore, the burning question is: what are we going to do about it?

The Washington Times
April 23, 2015

Limit government, grow America

Preceded by government growth under Presidents Theodore Roosevelt, Woodrow Wilson, Franklin Roosevelt and Lyndon Johnson, as well as the Sixteenth Amendment, six years of an Obama administration has turned the federal expanse into a terminal case of social, political, economic and national security disease.

Even though there was a revival under President Reagan and the Newt Gingrich congressional Contract with America (and the American people have since elected another Republican Congress to fight the liberal disease) President Obama has made it painfully clear that he will not be deterred from finishing his legacy terms in office, regardless of the consequences. Those consequences are forthcoming social, political, economic and national security disasters.

There is but one cure for these cancers, and that is to significantly reduce and limit the size, scope and power of government over our lives by electing a president and vice-president capable taking on the extremely difficult job of real leadership.

Indeed, "It's time for a change" is no longer a hackneyed phrase in these critical times of social, political, economic and moral decay brought on by the counter-cultural revolution of the 1960's. We must recover our social compatibility, political integrity, economic growth and military and foreign policy strength with true leadership that simply gets things done.

At this point in the 2016 presidential elections run-up, those leaders appear to be Wisconsin Gov. Scott Walker, Sen. Marco Rubio Florida Republican and Carly Fiorina. So, my fellow Americans, let's wake up and get it done for our survival and the survival of our nation – and recover the land of the free and home of the brave.

San Bernardino Sun
April 23, 2015

We must take action to counter terrorism

It is frightening to realize that the counter-culture, anti-establishment boomers of the 1960's and 70's have become an undermining threat to the survival of America from the shroud of the miseducation establishment, the tyranny of anti-Capitalism socialists, and the insidious growth of government.

Worse, the counter-cultural revolution has turned America into a superficial society of government dependency, social aggression, political hostility, relentlessly assaulted by selfish interests and the failures of good intentions.

It should be noted that Bill and Hillary Clinton are from the first of the Boomer generation, and President Obama is from the last of the generation. Enough said.

Indeed, our nation is steeped in uncertainty, and our freedom is fleeting from a deadly second front, which is being fatally demonstrated by the new barbarians on the block, who are the world-domination Jihadists of radical Islam [obsessed with eliminating non-believers from the face of the earth at any cost].

Alas, it has been said, and how true it is, that the only thing necessary for evil to triumph is for good people to remain silent and do nothing.

Therefore, the burning question is: what are we going to do about it?

VV Daily Press
April 17, 2015

Appeasing our enemies

President Obama is establishing a legacy replete with appeasing our enemies, (including Russia, while turning his back on Israel) reducing our national defense and neglecting our domestic defenses.

Indeed, there is no doubt that the president has maintained a dangerous hands-off reputation of ignoring Russian aggression against its neighbors, swelling ranks of radical Islamic terrorist aggression in the Middle East and Africa, and Iran's development of nuclear weapons.

Making matters worse, while President Obama is finishing fruitless negotiations with Iran, Russia is providing Iran with a missile defense system -- raising the serious possibility of Putin providing Iran with nuclear weapons -- while Iran takes over Yemen and expands its control throughout the Middle East.

Adding insult to injury, the president has appeased the Taliban with the irresponsible prisoner trade of 5 Taliban commanders, on his road to giving Afghanistan back to Taliban barbarians. And he has foolishly normalized relations with Castro's Communist Cuba 90 miles off our coast.

Coupled with a continuous pattern of seriously diminishing our economy, Mr. Obama is leading America on the road to ruin.

VV Daily Press
April 10, 2015

Internet service tax

President Obama's abuse of power continues unabated as he directs his EPA to enforce global warming edicts and his FCC Net Neutrality communications control, so it comes as no surprise that the FCC is gearing up to tax Internet services.

Indeed, California is the leader in punishing carbon taxation, gas taxes, online shopping taxes, public utility taxes and every conceivable form of taxation – which has obviously influenced the president, and will be welcomed by California government tax tyrants.

Surely, it has become painfully clear that unless voters turn things around, liberal Democrat regulation and tax tyranny will increase its heavy-handed, economy-busting rule over people's lives, and crush our future and the futures of our children. Enough is enough has already been surpassed.

VV Daily Press
April 6, 2015

Obama's deadly diplomatic fantasy

President Obama's deadly deal with devil in Iran is a diplomatic fantasy which will do nothing but buy Iran time to finish its nuclear weapons mission to destroy Israel, finish its domination of the Middle East, and turn its sights on attacking America and the West.

Indeed, who in their right mind could believe otherwise considering what Iran is doing right now with its tribal Shiite aggression against Sunni nations which will include Saudi Arabia, Egypt and Jordon?

Surely, Iran and other radical Islamic Jihadist elements are bent on ruling the Middle East and then turning their barbaric hatred against the United States – "The great Satan" – and other non-believers in the West with mass terrorism and nuclear weapons.

All because of Mr. Obama's fool's errand of accommodating complacency. Clearly, if we are to survive, we simply can't let that happen. Peace only comes from overwhelming strength and deterrence....

NewsMax Magazine
April 2015 Issue

ISIS' Bloody Savagery

It's become painfully clear that President Barack Obama has abdicated his role as the free world leader against radical Islamic terrorism by allowing the unholy war by evil savages against the good world to proliferate.

Contrary to what a State department spokeswoman recently said, ISIS atrocities simply cannot be countered by the ludicrous suggestion of getting them jobs. Moreover, ISIS is able to recruit disaffected young adults who don't need jobs.

Indeed, the unintended consequence of the failures of good intentions is not an option against terrorists. It's intentional insanity. ("ISIS Draws Europe's Teens," December).

VV Daily Press
March 29, 2015

AV Ranchos Water

Without naming names, liberal letter-writers who do little more than attack conservative letter-writers, and complain about the Daily Press, fail to appreciate the fact their letters are regularly published. The Daily Press is fair and balanced in that regard, unlike most liberal newspapers who seldom, if ever, publish conservative viewpoints. Being ungrateful is simply childish.

That aside, the main point of my letter is the issue of the Town of Apple Valley purchasing Ranchos Water. It appears to be somewhat of a toss-up. Our family has resided in Apple Valley since 1977. In balance, Apple Ranchos Water Company has performed well. Their rates have been fair, the system is well-maintained, and the company has been reliable including contracts and jobs.

Though the Town of Apple Valley has performed very well since incorporation, the Town's purchase of the company is questionable with too many unknowns. What is known is that too many municipalities that have taken over water companies have been abject failures. At this point I would say no to such a deal. Regardless, before the Town moves ahead with it, property-owning consumers should be allowed to vote on a matter of this importance to all residents.

VV Daily Press
March 27, 2015

Gov. Brown's Folly

Gov. Jerry Brown and the legislature cannot be trusted to ameliorate the water crisis with a $billion band-aid, or tapping into more of the $7.3 billion water bond approved by the voters in November unless the funds are used to improve the water system for real. Unfortunately, too many elected officials – and a few activist judges -- live in a political fantasyland, not in the real world of the people.

Instead, what is now needed is to either cancel Gov. Brown's $68-100 billion bullet train boondoggle and land-grab, or use the bond funds to address the drought and our water delivery in a meaningful, lasting manner. Clearly, if Central and Southern California dry up, it would be a train to nowhere.

In terms of the State Water Project delivering contracted water supplies to Central California farmers and Southern California consumers – paid for and maintained by property owners – we are to receive only 20% of our water allotment this year, up from our next-to-nothing 5% of our water allotment last year.

Indeed, much of that problem would be resolved by eliminating the extreme environmentalist federal court decision cutting 30% of our water from the Sacramento Delta to protect the tiny Delta Smelt at the expense of human health and welfare, and allowing millions of acre feet of our fresh water to flow wastefully to the ocean.

That is unconstitutional interference with private contracts for the sake of suicidal environmental insanity at the expense of crops, the California economy, and human life. Alas, the federal judge and Governor Brown might get the point if they were dropped out here in the middle of the Mojave Desert with half-full canteens of water....

Riverside Press Enterprise
March 25, 2015

Incompetent water managers

Gov. Jerry Brown and the legislature cannot be trusted to ameliorate the water crisis with a billion dollar Band-Aid, or tapping into more of the $7.3 billion water bond approved by the voters in November, unless the funds are used to improve the water system for real.

Unfortunately, too many elected officials (and activist judges) live in a political fantasyland, rather than in the real world.

Instead, what is now needed is to either cancel Brown's $68 billion bullet train boondoggle and land-grab, or use the bond funds to address the drought and our water delivery in a meaningful, lasting manner. Clearly, if Central and Southern California dry up, it would be a train to nowhere.

In terms of the State Water Project delivering contracted water supplies to Central California farmers and Southern California consumers (paid for and maintained by property owners): We are to receive only 20 percent of our water allotment this year, up from our next-to-nothing 5 percent of our water allotment last year.

Indeed, much of that problem would be resolved by eliminating the extreme environmentalist federal court decision cutting 30 percent of our water from the Sacramento Delta to protect the tiny Delta Smelt at the expense of human health and welfare, and allowing millions of acre-feet of our fresh water to flow wastefully to the ocean.

This is unconstitutional interference with private contracts for the sake of suicidal environmental insanity at the expense of crops, the California economy, and human life. Alas, the federal judge and Brown might get the point if they were dropped out here in the middle of the Mojave Desert with half-full canteens of water.

VV Daily Press
March 23, 2015

GOP letter to Iran is no mistake

The Daily Press "Controversy over Iran starts at top" – "Our View" editorial is very informative and hits the mark.

After failing miserably through over 6 years of dictatorial behavior administering domestic and foreign policy, President Obama continues his dangerous pursuits of circumventing the Constitution and Congress with punishing executive orders and blind diplomacy. Indeed, jamming feckless nuclear negotiations with an always insidious Iran down the throats of Israel, America and the world is simply the arrogant insanity of ignoring the inevitable consequences.

Surely, it was genuine patriotism – not a mistake – that drove the 47 GOP senators to write the strong letter to Iran, which should ultimately result in Congress imposing increased no nonsense sanctions, with the lead taken by President Obama, not the other way around. Clearly, we cannot make deals with the devil.

Certainly, President Obama treating Prime Minister Benjamin Netanyahu like an errant step-child was and is a monumental insult to the man, and the state of Israel. Indeed, it is more than evident that the president is undermining the re-election of prime minister in favor of a center-left leader, who if elected could very well cause Israel to be left in more danger of extinction, and America in more peril. We must support Netanyahu and Israel's survival.

Alas, the American people simply cannot assume a course of being socially, politically and economically naïve and expect to survive surging terrorism.

Riverside Press Enterprise
March 21, 2015

Obama's blinders on Israel

President Obama's history of treating Prime Minister Benjamin Netanyahu like an errant step-child was and is a monumental insult to the man, and the state of Israel.

Indeed, it is more than evident that the president attempted to undermine the re-election of the prime minister in favor of a center-left leader, who if elected would have caused Israel to be left in more danger of extinction, and America in more peril. We must support Netanyahu and Israel's survival.

Unfortunately, failing miserably through over 6 years of dictatorial behavior administering domestic and foreign policy, President Obama continues his dangerous pursuits of circumventing the Constitution and Congress with punishing executive orders and blind diplomacy.

Indeed, jamming feckless nuclear negotiations with an always insidious Iran down the throats of Israel, America and the world is simply the arrogant insanity of ignoring the inevitable consequences of misguided negotiations.

Surely, it was genuine patriotism – not a mistake – that drove the 47 GOP senators to write the strong letter to Iran, which should ultimately result in Congress imposing increased no nonsense sanctions, with the lead taken by President Obama, not the other way around. America cannot make deals with the devil.

Particularly, in this explosive era of Russian aggression, nuclear saber-rattling, North Korea and a Taliban Pakistan.

Moreover, ISIS is making it painfully clear that its extreme cancerous Jihad is metastasizing throughout the free world, radicalizing and exploiting enemies within.

Clearly, the American people and the West simply cannot assume a course of being socially, politically and economically naïve and expect to survive the malignant assaults of surging terrorism.

VV Daily Press
March 17, 2015

Gov. Brown's toy bullet train land fraud

Blinded by his pursuit of a high speed rail legacy, Governor Brown made an easy sell to naïve indoctrinated voters to take on escalating $billions in taxpayer bond debt for nothing more than buying Mr. Brown his toy bullet train from Northern to Southern California regardless of the enormous consequences.

Indeed, in the face of understandable resistance from Central Valley farmers who stand to lose and be cut-off from much needed farm lands, Brown's land grabbers are going full speed ahead with eminent domain fraud, not to mention the disruptive acquisitions to complete the needless train route.

Clearly, the California betrayal is deeply rooted with confiscatory taxation and regulations thrust upon businesses and the people by socialist government and environmentalistas responsible for cutting water to the California Water Project built and maintained by Central Valley farmers and Southern California property owners, exacerbated by the drought.

Coupled with making California an open-border sanctuary state, and opening prison gates to allow alien criminals to prey upon our citizens, Governor Brown, his elected administration and Democrats in the legislature should be recalled and given their permanent walking papers to run anywhere but California.

Enough is enough and beyond unconscionable.

Attention: Senators Boxer and Feinstein, California congressional democrats, and California AG Kamala Harris. You have also betrayed California.

VV Daily Press
March 16, 2015

California gas prices

California gas prices are up $1 in a month for unnecessary reasons: The Torrance refinery is shut down from damages and other refineries in the state are down to create the costly summer blend. Problem is, the state has refused to allow more refineries to be built. Indeed, with onerous restrictions against developing plentiful state oil and gas resources, our gas prices will continue to be the highest in the nation.

Worse, extreme California environmentalism is responsible for punishing AB-32 carbon taxes that not only raise the cost of gas, but raise the overall cost of living in the state. Coupled with environmentalist-caused high water prices and Central/Southern California water shortages, not from drought, and the insanity of big government over-regulation and taxes, California is sadly crashing in slow-motion.

Adding insult to injury, California being a sanctuary state for illegal aliens simply exacerbates the costs by $billions, along with the problems of domestic and national security.

VV Daily Press
March 13, 2015

First woman president

Editorial cartoonist, Lisa Benson – as usual -- hit the mark with her political sign, "Running from Hillary 2016."

Surely, former First lady (co-president), Senator and Secretary of State, Hillary Clinton has made it painfully clear that she is unquestionably entitled to inherit absolute power in Washington. Unfortunately, the first black president, Barack Obama, was an impulsive, costly mistake by the press and voters. Indeed, President Obama is establishing a painful legacy of unrelenting abuse of power.

Question is, will America make a worse mistake with the first woman president? Hopefully, the answer is a resounding, NO! Hillary

Clinton has a long record of political corruption and abuse of power, as evidenced by her sullied performance as first lady, U.S. Senator, and Secretary of State – which carelessly resulted in the terrorist murders of our Ambassador at Benghazi, Libya and three other Americans.

And the Hillary corruption chronicles continue as presidential candidate, unabated. Alas, the only alternative from the Democrat Party side appears to be extreme leftist, Senator Elizabeth Warren, which would be worse because she, along with Senator Bernie Sanders and President Obama, represent ERR, Evil Revenuers and Regulators -- demons who defame the name of the Democrat Party.

Clearly, the first woman president should be an honest, strong and productive woman of integrity such as Republicans, Carly Fiorina or Meg Whitman who genuinely represent the freedoms of our democratic republic.

VV Daily Press
March 12, 2015

President Obama vs. Israel

Re: "Netanyahu's visit highlights politics as usual" – editorial, March 3...

Speaker John Boehner was wise to have Israeli Prime Minister Netanyahu speak to Congress to address the truth about Iran's evil designs to rule the Middle East, backed by the force of nuclear weapons of mass destruction, and to advance their extremist Jihad against the world. Clearly, Prime Minister Netanyahu displayed candid courage in the face of being snubbed by President Obama and his Democrat minions, while his Secretary of State, John Kerry was busy capitulating to Iran's one-side negotiations.

Indeed, President Obama's passive legacy is on reckless course to disarm the United States in the face of dictator Vladimir Putin's Russian aggression, a rapidly expanding Islamic terrorist movement – and hapless negotiations with Iran's determination to become a nuclear weapons state, regardless of Prime Minister Netanyahu's real warnings – all of which threaten to annihilate Israel, America and the West.

Surely, Mr. Netanyahu is well known as a fearless defender of his homeland. And certainly, Israel will know if and when it's time to strike Iran to prevent their nuclear weapons capability, even though President Obama has wrongly warned them against unilateral action. Iran is a clear and present danger to Israel and our national security. The president and Congress must take decisive action or the consequences will be ours. Anything less is unacceptable.

Alas, though unthinkable, there is nothing to prevent Russia and/or North Korea from providing Iran with nuclear weapons.

San Bernardino Sun
March 11, 2015

Why California gas prices are so high

California gas prices are up $1 in a month for unnecessary reasons: The Torrance refinery is shut down from damages and other refineries in the state are down to create the costly summer blend.

The problem is, the state has refused to allow more refineries to be built. Indeed, with onerous restrictions against developing plentiful state oil and gas resources, our gas prices will continue to be the highest in the nation.

Worse, extreme California environmentalism is responsible for punishing AB 32 carbon taxes that not only raise the cost of gas, but raise the overall cost of living in the state. Coupled with environmentalist-caused high water prices and Central/Southern California water shortages, not from drought, and the insanity of big government over-regulation and taxes, California is sadly crashing in slow-motion.

Adding insult to injury, California being a sanctuary state for illegal aliens simply exacerbates the costs by $billions, along with the problems of domestic and national security.

Riverside Press Enterprise
March 10, 2015

Hillary's bid for president

Editorial cartoonist, Lisa Benson – as usual -- hit the mark with her political sign, "Running from Hillary 2016.

Surely, Hillary Clinton, the former First lady (co-president), senator and secretary of state has made it painfully clear that she is unquestionably entitled to inherit absolute power in Washington, D.C.

Unfortunately, the first black president, Barack Obama, was an impulsive, costly mistake by the press and voters. Indeed, President Obama is establishing a painful legacy of unrelenting abuse of power.

Will America make a worse mistake with the first woman president? Hillary Clinton has a long record of political corruption and abuse of power, as evidenced by her sullied performance as first lady, U.S. senator, and Secretary of State – which carelessly resulted in the terrorist murders of our ambassador and three other Americans stationed in Benghazi, Libya.

Alas, the only alternative from the Democratic Party side appears to be extreme leftist, Sen. Elizabeth Warren, D-Mass., which would be worse. Warren, along with Sen. Bernie Sanders, I-Vt., and Obama, represent Evil Revenuers and Regulators – the ERR -- demons who defame the name of the Democratic Party.

(Original letter)
First woman president

Editorial cartoonist, Lisa Benson – as usual -- hit the mark with her political sign, "Running from Hillary 2016.

Surely, former First lady (co-president), Senator and Secretary of State, Hillary Clinton has made it painfully clear that she is unquestionably entitled to inherit absolute power in Washington. Unfortunately, the first black president, Barack Obama, was an impulsive, costly mistake by the press and voters. Indeed, President Obama is establishing a painful legacy of unrelenting abuse of power.

Question is, will America make a worse mistake with the first woman president? Hopefully, the answer is a resounding, NO! Hillary Clinton has a long record of political corruption and abuse of power, as evidenced by her sullied performance as first lady, U.S. Senator, and Secretary of State – which carelessly resulted in the terrorist murders of our Ambassador at Benghazi, Libya and three other Americans.

And the Hillary corruption chronicles continue as presidential candidate, unabated. Alas, the only alternative from the Democrat Party side appears to be extreme leftist, Senator Elizabeth Warren, which would be worse because she, along with Senator Bernie Sanders and President Obama, represent ERR, Evil Revenuers and Regulators -- demons who defame the name of the Democrat Party.

Clearly, the first woman president should be an honest, strong and productive woman of integrity such as Republicans, Carly Fiorina or Meg Whitman who genuinely represent the freedoms of our democratic republic.

Los Angeles Times
March 7, 2015

Netanyahu's Speech

Daniel B. Jeffs of Apple Valley says Obama is leaving a dangerous legacy:

Speaker John A. Boehner (R-Ohio) was wise to have Netanyahu speak to Congress about Iran's evil designs to rule the Middle East, backed by the force of nuclear weapons. Clearly, Netanyahu displayed candid courage in the face of being snubbed by Obama and his Democratic minions.

Indeed, Obama is on reckless course to disarm the United States in the face of Iran's determination to become a nuclear weapons state, regardless of Netanyahu's warnings.

Surely, Mr. Netanyahu is well known as a fearless defender of his homeland. And certainly, Israel will know if and when it's time to strike Iran to prevent their nuclear weapons capability.

Alas, though unthinkable, there is nothing to prevent North Korea from providing Iran with nuclear weapons.

VV Daily Press
March 6, 2015

President and leftist Dems

ObamaCare, ObamaFinance, ObamaEnergy, and now the ObamaNet are making it painfully clear that President Obama's ObamAmerica and leftist Democrats – including Hollywood -- are the party of tyranny against the best interests of the American people with destructive regulations, punishing taxation and unsustainable national debt.

Worse, President Obama's legacy is on reckless course to disarm the United States in the face of dictator Putin's Russian aggression, a rapidly expanding Islamic terrorist movement – and feigned negotiations with Iran's nuclear weapons state, regardless of Israeli Prime Minister Netanyahu's real warnings and self-defense – all of which threaten to annihilate Israel, America and the West.

Clearly, it's bad enough that the counter-culture revolutionists have turned our country into a superficial society of social injustice, political chaos, selfish interests, economic instability, steeped in uncertainty, and extremes.Indeed, the Boomer generation is now well on the way to overwhelming Medicare after developing a nation of fools by indoctrination, distractions, deceptions, lies, the insidious intended consequences of failed good intentions, and the loss of freedoms. That is what a socialist takeover is all about.

Alas, the next two years will be our nation's reckoning with the enemy within the 7th round of President Obama and his minions vs. America, with only the Republican Party and the informed people standing in the way of an 8th round knockout.Surely, Mr. Obama's White House is a "House of Cards" stain on the presidency. Attention: Republican Congress, governors and presidential nominee! Strong language and action is what is needed -- for our survival and restoration. The washed-out Washington way simply won't cut it!

The Washington Times
March 4, 2015

Netanyahu right on Iran

House Speaker Boehner was wise to have Israeli Prime Minister Benjamin Netanyahu speak to Congress to address the truth about Iran's evil designs to rule the Middle East. Prime Minister Netanyahu displayed candid courage in the face of being snubbed by President Obama and his Democrat minions, while his Secretary of State, John Kerry was busy capitulating to Iran's one-side negotiations.

Indeed, President Obama's passive legacy is on reckless course to disarm the United States in the face of dictator Vladimir Putin's aggression, a rapidly expanding Islamic terrorist movement and hapless negotiations with Iran (regardless of Prime Minister Netanyahu's warnings) all of which threaten to annihilate Israel, America and the West.

Surely, Mr. Netanyahu is well known as a fearless defender of his homeland. And certainly, Israel will know if and when it's time to strike Iran to prevent their nuclear weapons capability, even though Mr. Obama has wrongly warned them against unilateral action.

Iran is a clear and present danger to Israel and our national security. The president and Congress must take decisive action or the consequences will be ours. Anything less is unacceptable. Alas, though unthinkable, there is nothing to prevent Russia and/or North Korea from providing Iran with nuclear weapons.

VV Daily Press
March 1, 2015

President Obama's poison pens

President Obama's executive order and administration arrogance continues with a Keystone Pipeline veto against the economy, and his FCC move under the guise of Net Neutrality to control the Internet and squelch free speech.

Indeed, it's bad enough that Mr. Obama's poison executive order pen – and now his poison veto pen -- have been working overtime against our energy and our economy. But when he moves to control our freedom of communications over the internet, coupled with his undue influence over the news media, our liberty is threatened.

Worse, it is well known and understood that this president has surrendered our national security to Islamic terrorism, Russian aggression and the inevitability of a nuclear weaponized Iran. And, coupled with his reckless reductions of our military and nuclear strength, the real clear and present danger to America has become President Obama and his minions.

Adding insult to injury, California's government abuse of power and environmental extremists exacerbates the plight of the people with land-grabs, over-regulation, punishing taxation, dangerous water shortages, costly illegal immigrant sanctuary, and the escalation of crime.

Fortunately, we still have the right to voter initiative, referendum and recall, which will extend the July deadline and give us the chance to keep our plastic grocery bags with a win in the November 2016 election.

VV Daily Press
February 25, 2015

Re: Al Vogler - Valley Voices
Daily Press Opinion, Feb 22, 2015

Water crisis runs deep

Al Vogler's concerns are shared by all Southern California property owners who paid for and maintain the California Water Project, which was constructed to provide Sacramento Delta Northern California water resources to millions of water users in Southern California – particularly, after suffering years of drought conditions.

However, even after the recent rains, the man-made drought continues because of the Natural Resources Defense Council extremists and a federal judge cutting water supplies nearly in half to protect the tiny Delta Smelt fish at the expense of human health and welfare.

Of course this has resulted in the constant and unnecessary dumping millions of acre-feet of fresh water into the sea, which should have been going to quench the thirst of farms and water users in Central and Southern California.

As a 2007/2008 county grand jury member, my committee investigated county water resources from several California Water Project contractors among those who service water contracts from the Project throughout Southern California.

As a result of my investigation, I was clearly outraged by the fact that the federal judge and other state water authorities have seriously and continuously violated the Constitution's prohibition of government interference with private contracts.

Indeed, it should be strongly suggested that the California Water Project Contractors Association and/or property owner users -- of which I am one – file state and federal lawsuits to restore all Project water resources cut off by the federal court at the behest of extremist groups and supported by state and federal officials. The Constitution certainly demands it.

The Washington Times
February 25, 2015

Oscars miss the mark again

The 2015 Academy Awards was simply the final round of Hollywood celebrating itself again – and again and again. Alas, with few exceptions, the film and entertainment industry continues to decline into little more than sex, violence, shallow stories, lack of imagination and original thought reduced to narcissism resembling "Fifty Shades of Grey."

As for the exceptions, mostly-true stories such as "Selma," "The Theory of Everything," "The imitation Game," "Foxcatcher," "American Sniper," "Still Alice," "Boyhood," and "Whiplash" rounded out the exceptions. However, "Birdman or (The unexpected Virtue of Ignorance)" overshadowed them all with the darkness of mass neurosis that consumes the hopelessly self-involved. "Best Picture" and "Best Director"? Hardly.

Certainly, the only clarity coming from the Oscars dog-and-pony costume show was the host with least, Neil Patrick Harris, those promoting liberal social and political issues and the whiners. Snubbing the genuine talent and integrity of the real best director, Clint Eastwood, epitomizes the intolerance and the ongoing lack of morality that is Hollywood.

However the name fits. Holly is supposed to be a symbol of joy – yet its leaves are extremely prickly, guarding a soul of wood. Society needs a do-over.

Commentary
By Daniel B. Jeffs

VV Daily Press
Commentary
February 24, 2015

Hollywood celebrating itself, again....

The 2015 Academy Awards was simply the final round of Hollywood celebrating itself again, and again, and again.... Alas, with few exceptions, the film and entertainment industry continues to decline into little more than sex, violence, shallow stories, lack of imagination and original thought reduced to fifty shades of grey narcissism.

As for the exceptions, mostly-true stories such as "Selma," "The Theory of Everything," "The imitation Game," "Foxcatcher" and "American Sniper" – and "Still Alice," "Boyhood," plus "Whiplash" – rounded out the exceptions. However, "Birdman or (The unexpected Virtue of Ignorance)" over-shadowed them all with the darkness of mass neurosis that consumes the hopelessly self-involved. Best Picture and Best Director? Hardly.

Certainly, the only clarity coming from the Oscars dog and pony costume show was the host with least, those promoting liberal social and political issues, and the whiners. Snubbing the genuine talent and integrity of the real best director, Clint Eastwood, is the intolerance and the ongoing lack of morality that is Hollywood.

However the name fits. Holly is supposed to be a symbol of joy – yet it's leaves are extremely prickly, guarding a soul of wood. Society needs a do-over.

Daniel B. Jeffs

VV Daily Press
February 23, 2015

Community organizing not the answer

Contrary to President Obama's naïve experience with community organizing, his feckless global summit focusing on the empowerment of local communities to counter the violent extremism of ISIS, al-Qaeda and other Islamic terrorists with social justice, strong leadership, families, opportunity, education, economic improvement and jobs is simply ludicrous.

Certainly, decades of the failed war on poverty and community organizing resulted in the unresolved liberal government's proliferation of disorganized, disoriented, irresponsible welfare neighborhoods, miseducation, single mothers, absent fathers, drugs, gangs, violent crime and perpetual anger in vulnerable American communities, which are living proof that it doesn't work.

Alas, it's become painfully clear that President Obama has abdicated his role as the free world leader against radical Islamic terrorism by allowing the not holy, but unholy war by evil savages against the good world to proliferate. Indeed, the unintended consequence of the failures of good intentions is not an option against terrorists bent on world domination. It's intentional insanity.

San Diego Union-Tribune
February 22, 2015

Unions hurt economy and themselves

The selfish interests of striking dockworker union bosses at California and West Coast ports are simply being self-destructive for their union members, and damaging to thousands of other workers, local and state businesses, their employees, and the overall California and U.S. economy.

That's simply insane in these perilous economic times. Alas, that seems to be the long-term negative destiny caused by California's intrusive liberal government's social, political, and economic disservice to the people of the state and the nation.

(original letter)

Unions are damaging themselves and the California economy
The selfish interests of striking dockworker union bosses at California and West Coast ports are simply being self-destructive for their union members, and damaging to thousands of other workers, local and state businesses, their employees, and the overall California and U.S. economy.

That's simply insane in these perilous economic times. Alas, that seems to be the long-term negative destiny caused by California's intrusive liberal government's social, political, and economic disservice to the people of the state and the nation.

Indeed, it's far past time to get out of reckless and costly union traps and get in to economic freedom and the right to work.

Riverside Press Enterprise
February 21, 2015
(lead letter)

Allowing ISIS to flourish

President Obama has abdicated his role as the leader of the free world. He has allowed an unholy war by evil savages against the good world to proliferate.

Contrary to what a State department spokeswoman recently said, Islamic State atrocities simply cannot be countered by the ludicrous suggestion of getting them jobs.

Indeed, the unintended consequence of the failures of good intentions is not an option against terrorists. It's intentional insanity.

VV Daily Press
February 19, 2015

ISIS atrocities a holy war?

It's become painfully clear that President Obama has abdicated his role as the free world leader against radical Islamic terrorism by allowing the, not holy, but unholy war by evil savages against the good world to proliferate. Contrary to what a State department spokeswoman recently said, ISIS atrocities simply cannot be countered by the ludicrous suggestion of getting them jobs. Indeed, the unintended consequence of the failures of good intentions is not an option against terrorists. It's intentional insanity.

VV Daily Press
February 11, 2015

Senator Feinstein's monuments

Senator Dianne Feinstein is at it again by introducing legislation that would increase federal control over 1.6 million acres of our Mojave Desert.

It was bad enough that Feinstein picked up former senator Cranston's efforts against the desert, but she apparently won't be satisfied until she established absolute federal power over our lands.

Worse, President Obama is bound and determined to do the same thing throughout the country, particularly seizing power over our natural resources such as coal, oil and all mining.

Indeed, abuse of power has become a standard practice for Mr. Obama in his efforts to fundamentally transform America to fit his ideology, regardless of how it affects our economy and our freedoms.

A citizen's word of advice to President Obama, Senator Feinstein and intrusive government, including California's government: Keep your noses out of our business, our lives and our liberty. And keep in mind what "local control" means to the states and the people.

Monuments are only for people who earn it.

NEWSMAX Magazine
February issue 2015

Race tensions rise

After decades of progress, race relations are obviously worse since President Obama was elected and became an imperial president ("Success wins over black victimhood," December 2014).

Race relations will certainly deteriorate even further as the protests continue and grow throughout the country, invading streets, highways and freeways, blocking traffic and endangering the public. President Obama should step-up to improve race relations as a major part of his legacy. If not, the insanity goes on, unabated.

Lest we forget, the police are our first line of defense in neighborhoods, communities, and cities against criminals and terrorists.

(original letter)

Race relations in America

After decades of progress, race relations are obviously worse since President Obama was elected and became an imperial president, to the extent of giving African-Americans an arrogant superiority complex and/or being treated as sacred cows in the Obama era. Indeed, Hollywood and advertisers have responded by over-representing blacks in films, television and commercials.

Worse, racial protests, demonstrations, rioting, arson and looting have been exacerbated by President Obama, his aggressively radical race counselor, Al Sharpton, indoctrinated college students and the complicit news media -- touched off by the Travon Martin case -- then magnified by the Michael Brown and Eric Garner death cases at the hands of police -- who were not indicted by local grand juries.

Race relations will certainly deteriorate even further as the protests continue and grow throughout the country, invading streets, highways and freeways, blocking traffic and endangering the public -- even blocking Christmas shoppers in stores and malls. President Obama should step-up to improve race relations as a major part of his legacy. If not, the insanity goes on, unabated......

Lest we forget, the police are our first line of defense in neighborhoods, communities and cities against criminals and terrorists.

Commentary
By Daniel B. Jeffs

VV Daily Press
Commentary
February 24, 2015

Hollywood celebrating itself, again….

The 2015 Academy Awards was simply the final round of Hollywood celebrating itself again, and again, and again…. Alas, with few exceptions, the film and entertainment industry continues to decline into little more than sex, violence, shallow stories, lack of imagination and original thought reduced to fifty shades of grey narcissism.

As for the exceptions, mostly-true stories such as "Selma," "The Theory of Everything," "The imitation Game," "Foxcatcher" and "American Sniper" – and "Still Alice," "Boyhood," plus "Whiplash" – rounded out the exceptions. However, "Birdman or (The unexpected Virtue of Ignorance)" over-shadowed them all with the darkness of mass neurosis that consumes the hopelessly self-involved. Best Picture and Best Director? Hardly.

Certainly, the only clarity coming from the Oscars dog and pony costume show was the host with least, those promoting liberal social and political issues, and the whiners. Snubbing the genuine talent and integrity of the real best director, Clint Eastwood, is the intolerance and the ongoing lack of morality that is Hollywood.

However the name fits. Holly is supposed to be a symbol of joy – yet it's leaves are extremely prickly, guarding a soul of wood. Society needs a do-over.

Daniel B. Jeffs

Riverside Press Enterprise
January 22, 2015

Obama's State of the Union fails to deliver

President Obama's state of the union speech was little more than preaching to the choir of Democrats, lecturing Republicans, taking credit for the improved economy and insisting on more regulation, taxing and spending. The truth is, the economy has improved not because of Mr. Obama, but in spite of him.

Alas, the president's sorry state of the union and his legacy is replete with government growth, enormous debt, economic stagnation and diminishing national security.

Hopefully, the economy won't collapse and America will not be rife with terrorism during President Obama's last two years in office.

Daniel B. Jeffs
Apple Valley

USA TODAY
January 22, 2015
Opinion – Your Say
State of the Union
(Lead letter with headline)

Is the economy better because of Obama or despite him?

President Obama's state of the union speech was little more than preaching to the choir of Democrats and lecturing Republicans. Obama took credit for the improved economy and backed more regulation, taxing and spending ("Obama pushes plans to hoist middle class," News, Wednesday),

The truth is, the economy has improved not because of Obama, but in despite him. Alas, the president's sorry speech and his legacy are replete with government growth, enormous debt, economic stagnation and diminishing national security.

Hopefully, the economy won't collapse and America will not be rife with terrorism during President Obama's last two years in office.

Daniel B. Jeffs
Apple Valley, Calif.

Riverside Press Enterprise
January 19, 2015

Call it what it is: Treason

An Ohio man, and radicalized Muslim convert, Christopher Cornell, was arrested for plotting to attack the capitol.

This is a treasonous plot to overthrow our government, but he will undoubtedly no be charged with treason. Others who should be charged with treason include Major Nidal Hasan, Sgt, Bowe Burgdahl, Pvt. Chelsea Manning, Edward Snowden, American Muslim imams who support arming the Islamic State in Iraq and Syria, and all the American citizens who went to fight with ISIS.

But they won't be.

This is particularly the case with President Obama and Attorney General Eric Holder in office, who fail to support and defend the Constitution and the United States against all enemies, foreign and domestic. No one has been charged with treason for many years.

Why?

This is a serious matter that should be looked into by our elected representatives and the media. Our survival is at stake.

The Washington Times
January 13, 2015

Paris no-show matches rest of presidency

President Obama's failure last week to make an appearance joining world leaders in solidarity against the terrorist attacks in Paris highlighted six years of failed leadership ("Obama's snub of Paris," Jan, 12) This failure resulted in the unfettered growth of al Qaeda and Islamic State terrorists throughout the Middle East, Africa and the World, and puts America and the West at extreme risk.

Worse, the president's failure to secure Iraq and stop Iran from obtaining nuclear weapons, as well as its implicit permission of the Taliban to take Pakistan (which could result in Taliban takeover of Pakistan and the country's nuclear weapons) makes Israel, India and the United States vulnerable to nuclear attacks.

Indeed, Mr. Obama's failure to execute a firm plan to secure our borders and fight terrorism wherever it raises its evil head will likely result in small terrorist cells spread throughout the United States. These cells could result in nationwide attacks on Americans. Hopefully, those terrorist cells are not already in place.

Toying with terrorism, coupled with the president's failure to maintain or increase our nuclear defenses and the defense of our allies makes it painfully clear Mr. Obama has abdicated his solemn responsibility to protect and defend our nation from all enemies, foreign and domestic.

Los Angeles Times
January 11, 2015

Alternative ways to go green

The Times' support of Gov. Brown's costly green agenda comes as no surprise. Indeed, it doesn't seem to matter how much damage the punishing cap and trade taxes will do to California's economy in terms of skyrocketing energy prices and the overall cost of living.

Coupled with all the damage California's U.S. Senator Barbara Boxer has done with her environmental extremist work against California, she and Gov. Brown have blindly driven California on a runaway train to crashing at the hands of regressive liberals.

(original letter)

Re: Gov. Brown's green agenda – editorial
and Sen. Boxer's exit

The Los Angeles Times editorial board's support of Gov. Brown's costly green agenda comes as no surprise. Indeed, it doesn't seem to matter how much damage AB 32's punishing cap and trade taxes will do to California's economy or to the people of California in terms of skyrocketing energy prices and the overall cost of living. The L.A. Times supports it along with the Democrat Legislature in terms of global warming hoax and unreliable green energy.

Coupled with all the damage California's U.S. Senator Barbara Boxer has done with her environmental extremist work against California and the nation, Sen. Boxer and Gov. Brown have blindly driven California on a runaway train to crashing at the hands of regressive liberals. Alas, at least we can finally be rid of authoritarian hand when she leaves the Senate. Still, we will continue to be assaulted and battered by Gov. Brown's tax lies and high speed rail money pit.

Unfortunately, Sen. Boxer and soon-to-retire Sen. Feinstein will surely be replaced with the like infections of regressive Democrats elected by indoctrinated voters bent on committing voter-assisted social, political and economic suicide..

San Bernardino Sun
January 8, 2015

New year of life, liberty and pursuit of happiness

The best New Year's resolution would be for the American people to resolve to fight-off the socialist cancer metastasizing throughout the body of our society from the attacks against the Founders' traditional America, our Constitution and free markets, the abuse of power by big government – complicit news media and entertainment industry -- to badly misinformed parenting, to students being indoctrinated by the miseducation system in factories of ignorance, to anti-social media, and the relentless spread of mind-numbing propaganda and criminal behavior.

Indeed, 2015 should be embraced by getting our lives together for life, liberty, the pursuit of happiness -- and the defense of our domestic and national security freedom.